REVERIES

RODIN

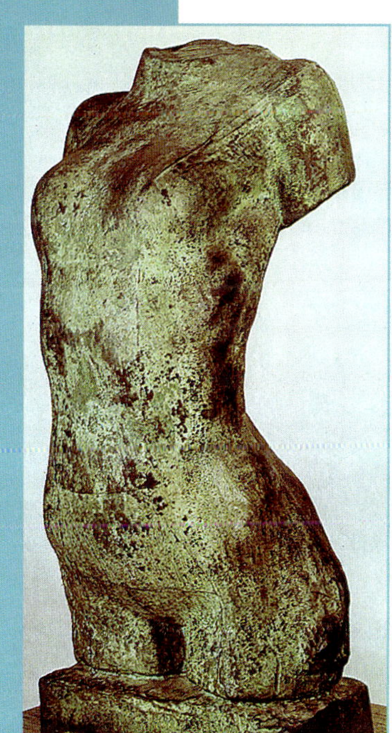

Tom Parsons

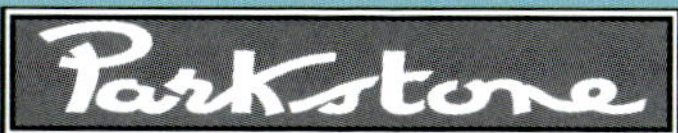

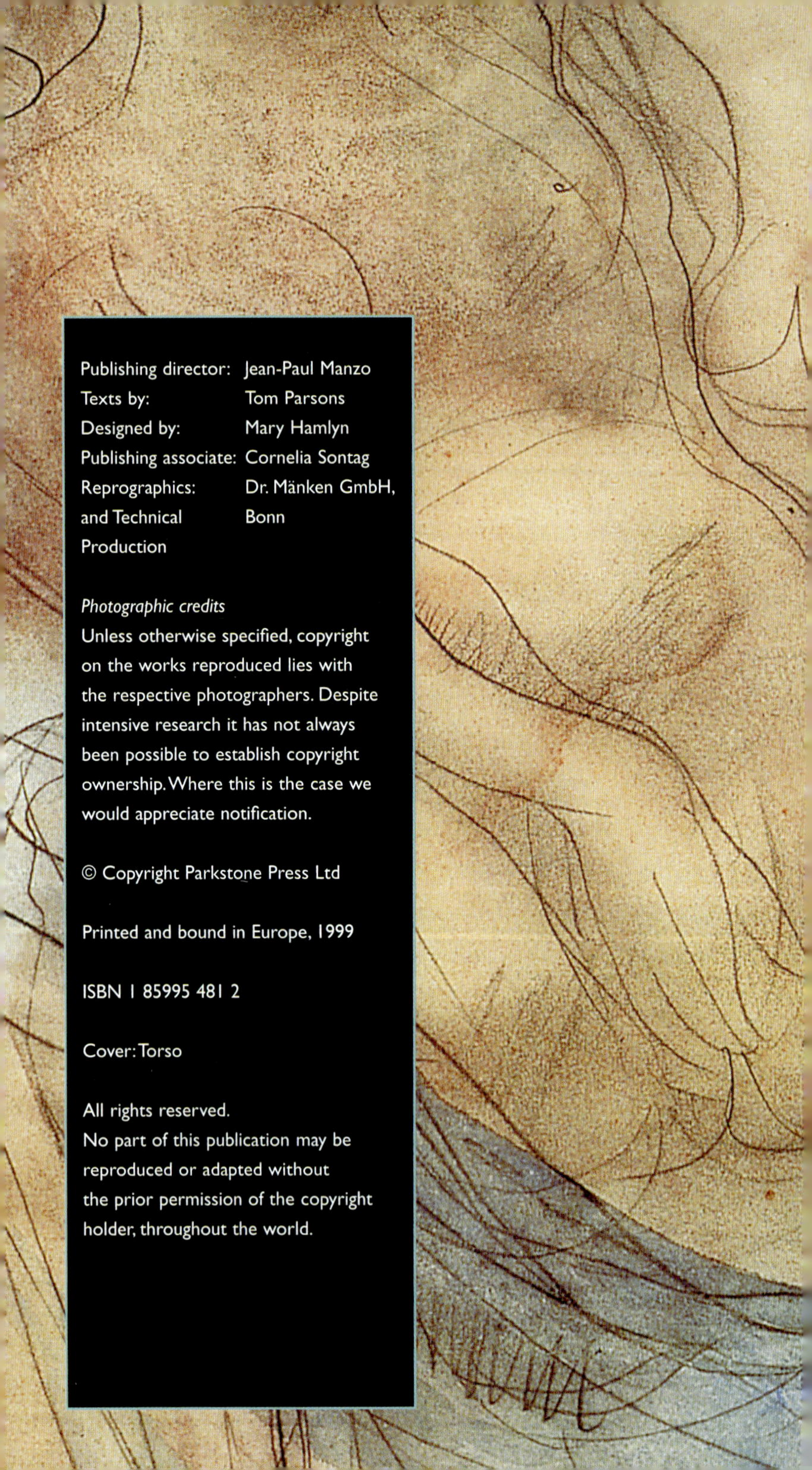

Publishing director: Jean-Paul Manzo
Texts by: Tom Parsons
Designed by: Mary Hamlyn
Publishing associate: Cornelia Sontag
Reprographics: and Technical Production: Dr. Mänken GmbH, Bonn

Photographic credits
Unless otherwise specified, copyright on the works reproduced lies with the respective photographers. Despite intensive research it has not always been possible to establish copyright ownership. Where this is the case we would appreciate notification.

Printed and bound in Europe, 1999

ISBN 1 85995 481 2

Cover: Torso

RODIN

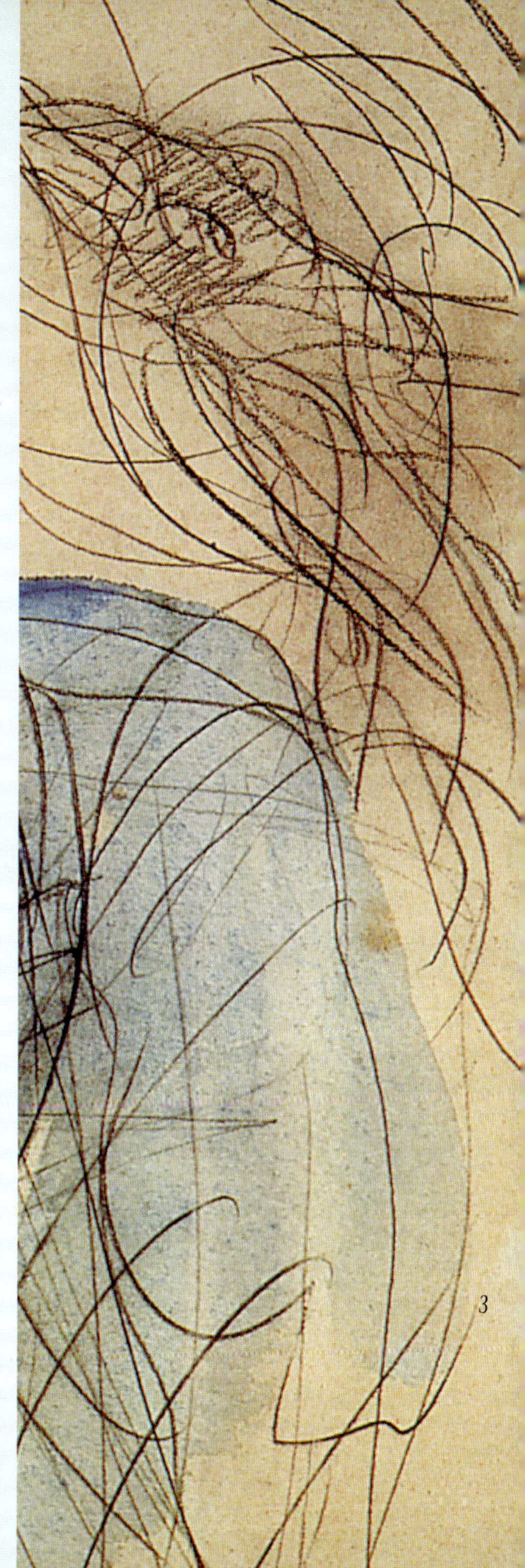

At the principal annual art exhibition, the Salon, in Paris in 1898, the sculptor Auguste Rodin exhibited two enormous statues - *The Kiss* (1) and *Balzac* (2). He was fifty eight years old and nearing the height of his fame. It was both a challenging gesture and a typically brave response to professional and private adversity. Originally the embracing couple in *The Kiss* had been

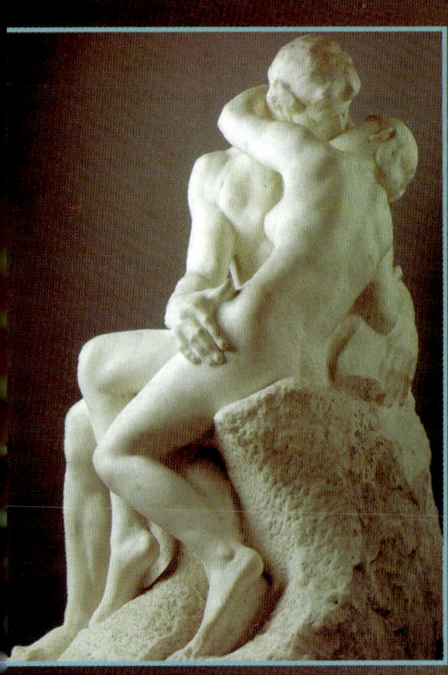

1 The Kiss

envisaged on a much smaller scale to take their place on a massive pair of doors commissioned from the French government for a projected new museum of decorative art. Rodin had been working on the doors, known as the *Gates of Hell* (3), for almost twenty years; but by 1898 it had become clear that the museum would not be built. That year Rodin enlarged the couple massively in marble for the Salon. The Balzac sculpture was another failed public monument, initially

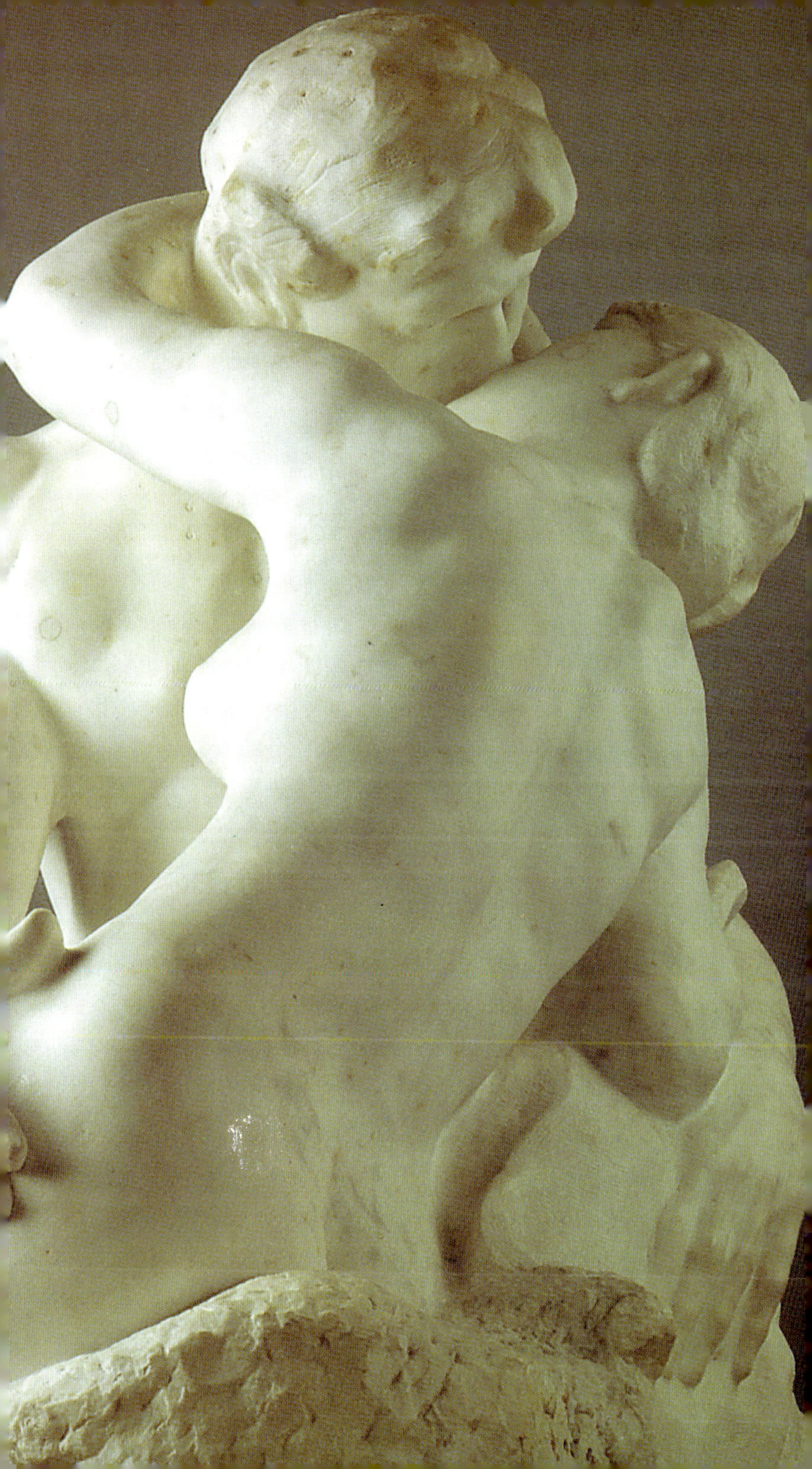

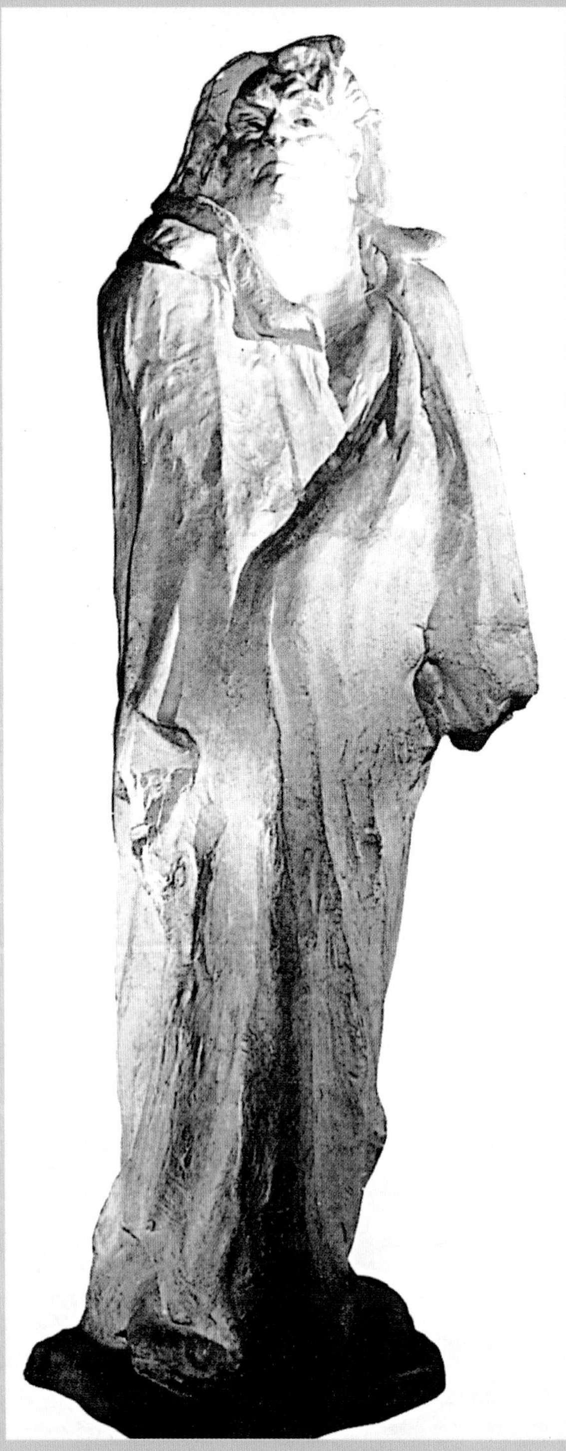

commissioned by a literary society in 1891 to commemorate the titanic nineteenth-century writer. After seven years of preparatory study Rodin had decided to exhibit the work to reassure his critics that the project was near completion. When the committee responsible for the work saw it at the Salon, roughly cast in plaster, they rejected it and terminated their contract with him.

These were the professional difficulties facing the sculptor. Privately, Rodin's lover Camille Claudel, had just ended their relationship. Both sets of troubles, emotional and artistic, will be considered later. Certainly both works, so antithetical in style, discharge conspicuous erotic energies - a blatant indication that this element of the erotic, of sensual force and sexual primacy were central to Rodin's life and work.

2 Balzac, marble.

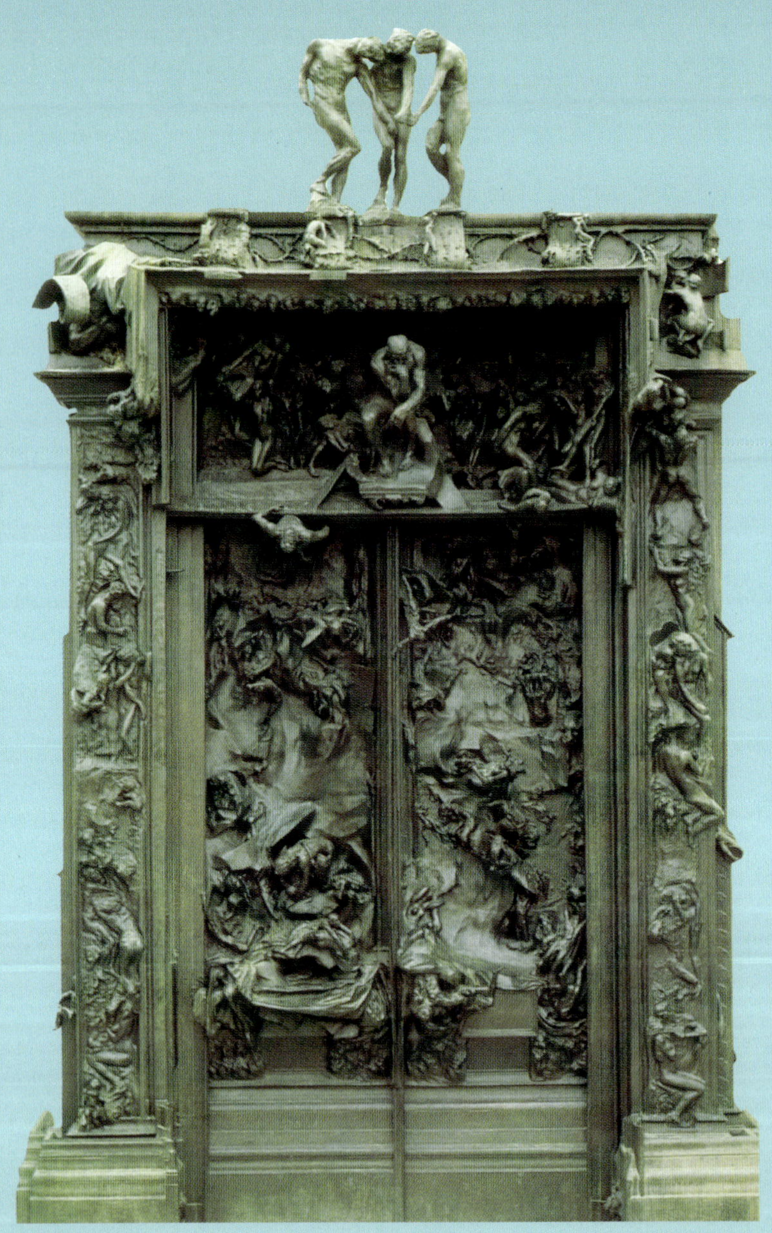

8

Of course the differences between the two works are immediately the more striking. If it still surprises us to know that both these works were made by the same man, the well-dressed Parisian crowds who saw them prominently on view at the Salon were equally, if not more, non-plussed. *The Kiss* is smoothly carved in

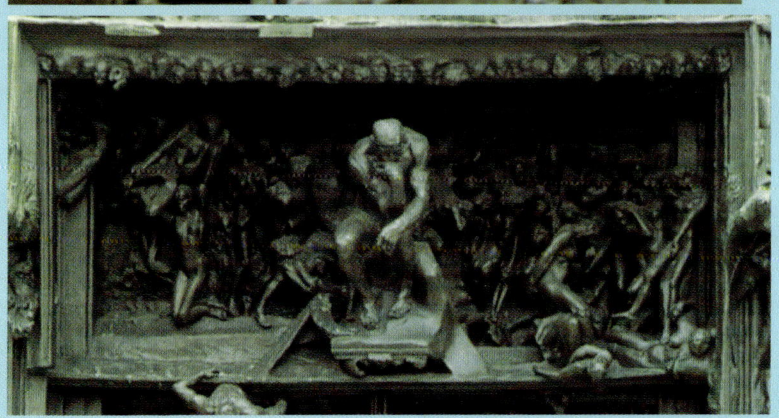

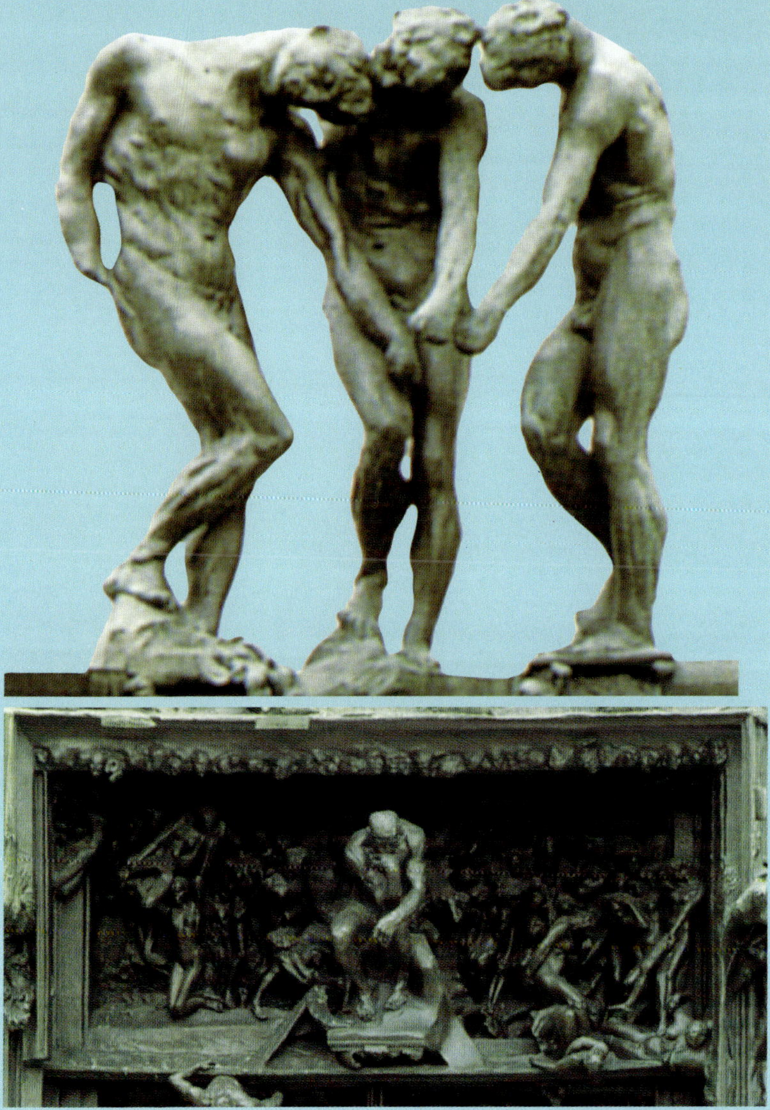

3 Gates of Hell.

gleaming white marble, its massive lovers presented as idealized and divinely beautiful protagonists. *The Balzac* on the other hand, crudely cast in plaster (other versions in bronze and marble were made later), is powerfully ugly, with its jagged profiles, rough textures and a more or less complete disregard for anatomical detail,

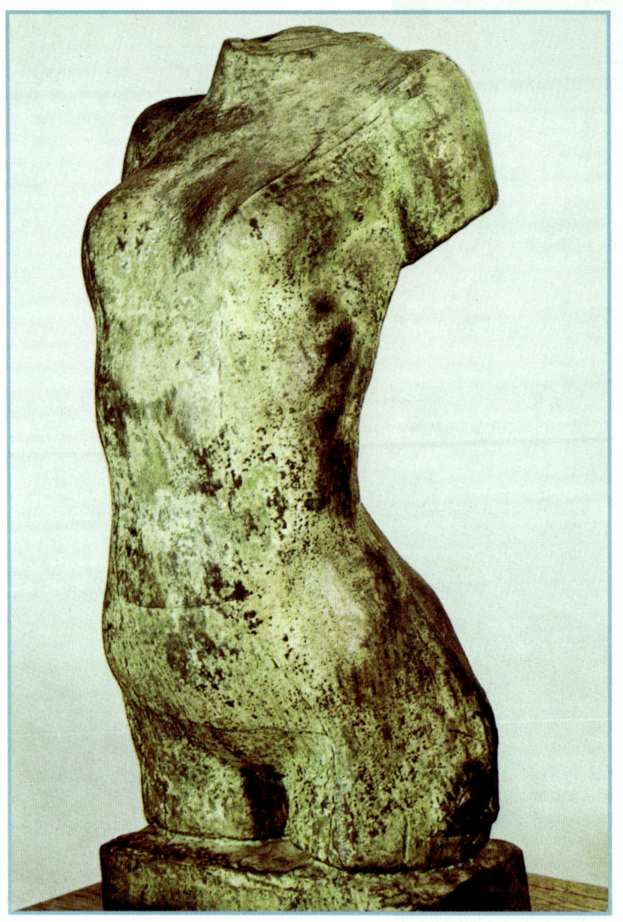

accuracy and finish. In *The Kiss* the entwined couple enact a titillating, almost comic encounter. The figures were originally inspired by Dante's lovers Paolo and Francesca, damned eternally for incest, but here revealing nothing of their awful, poetic fate (Rodin made another, darker version for the doors - 17). It is the woman who has initiated proceedings - while she forthrightly embraces her lover and has moved her right leg over onto his lap, he only tentatively touches her left hip. (In his own love affairs it was usually Rodin who made the

4 Torso of a Young Woman, bronze

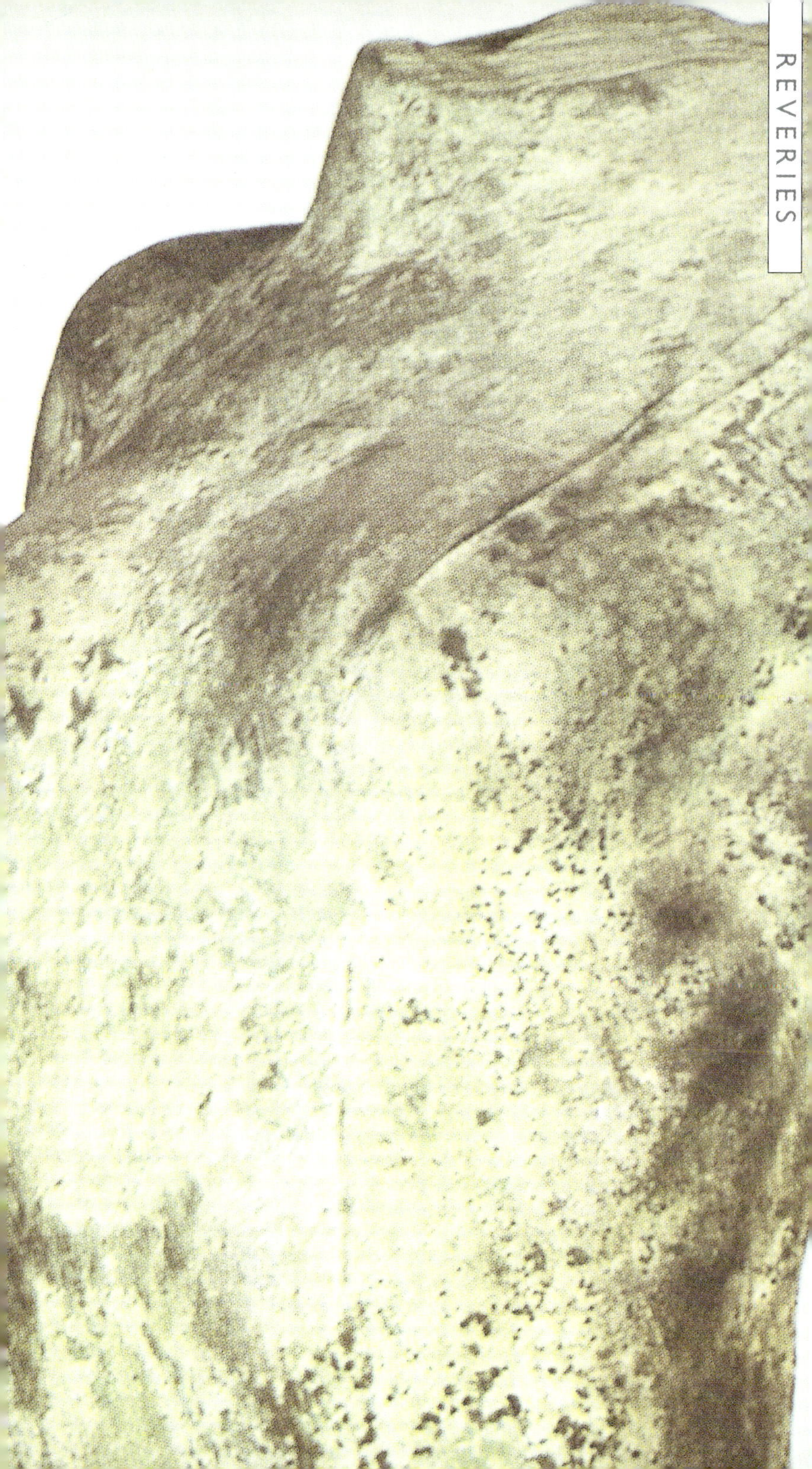

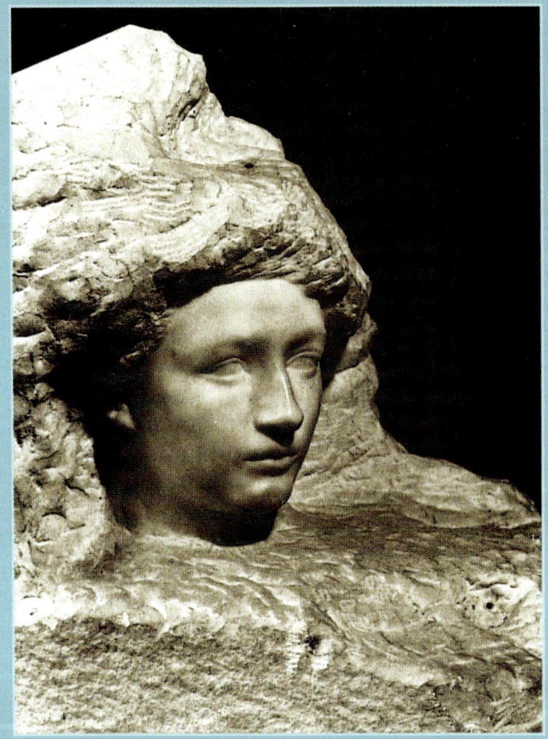

5 Dawn

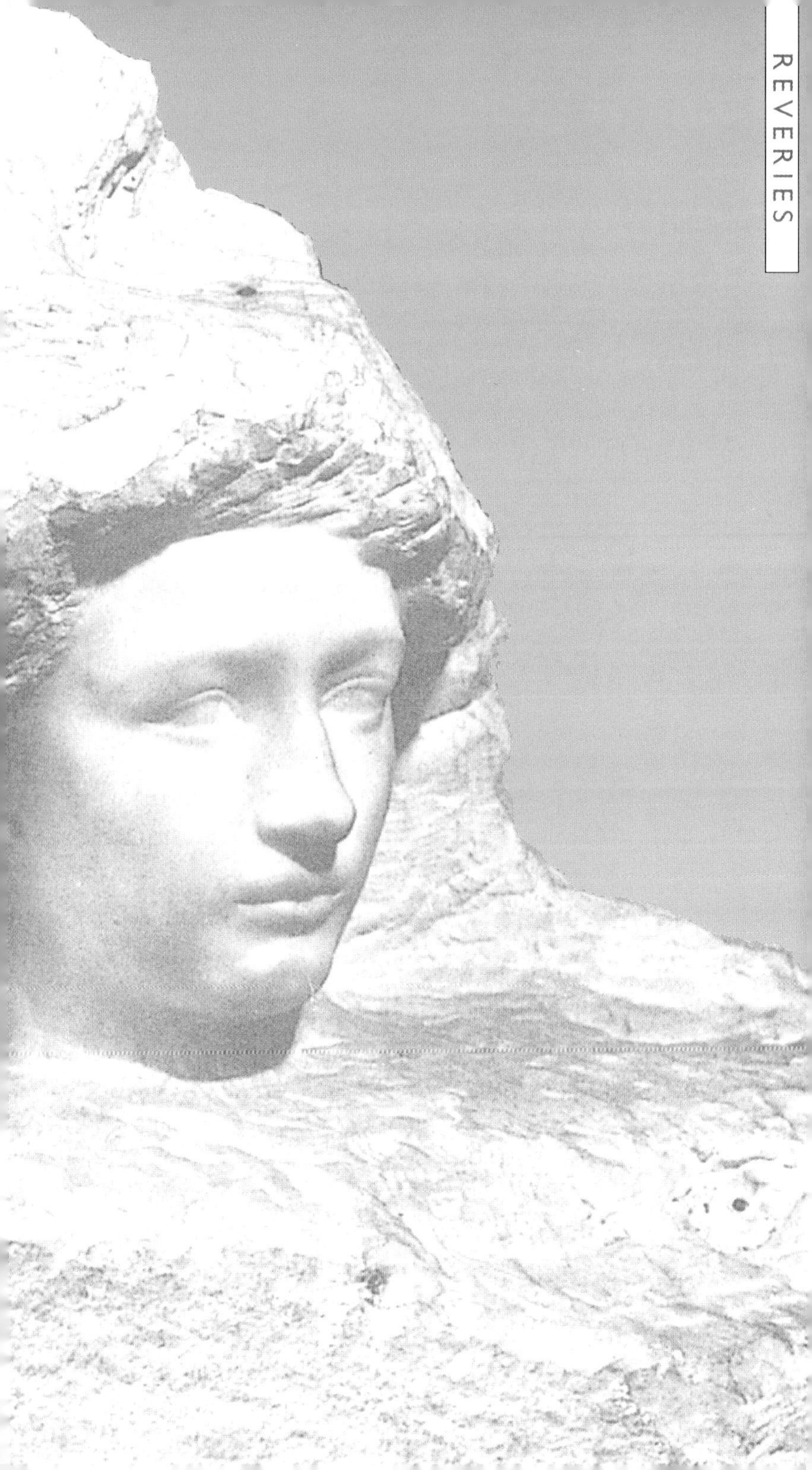

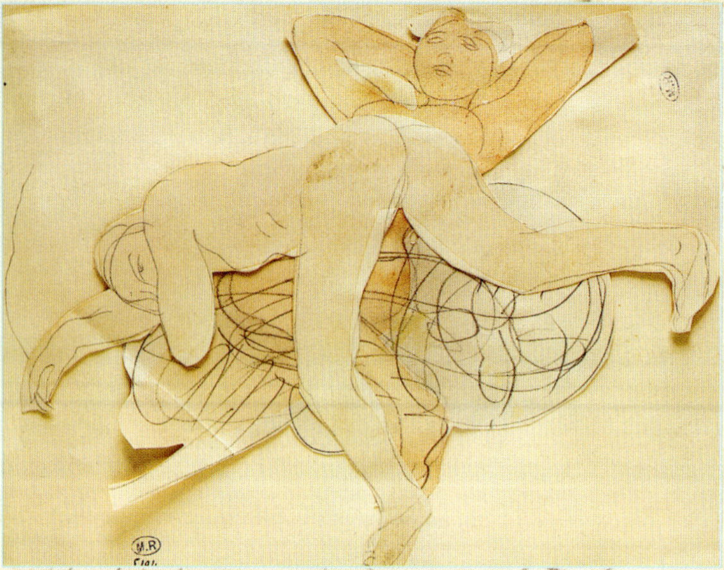

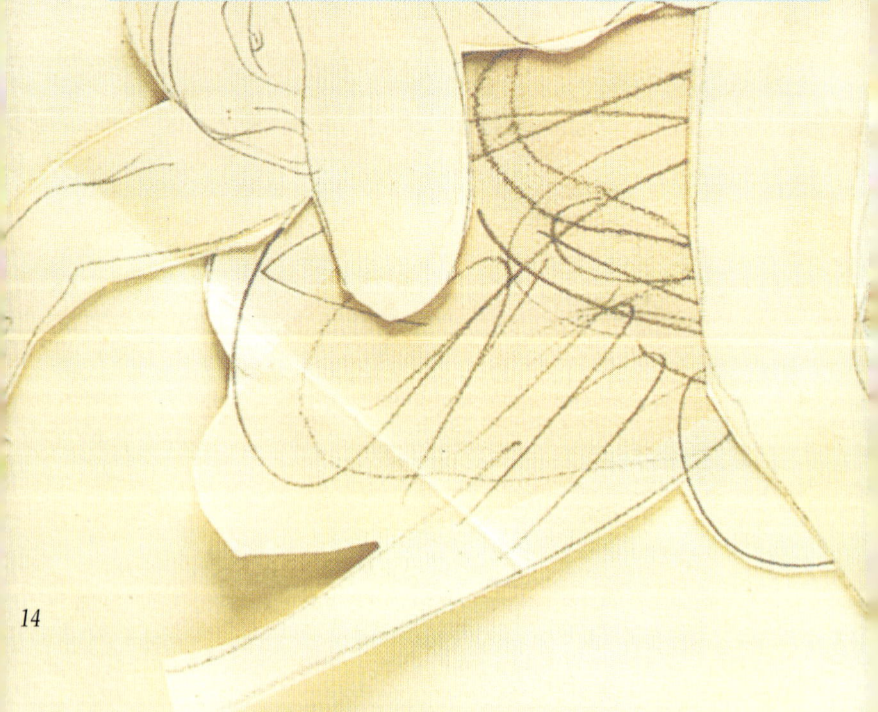

6 Sapphic couple lying near a wheel of fortune

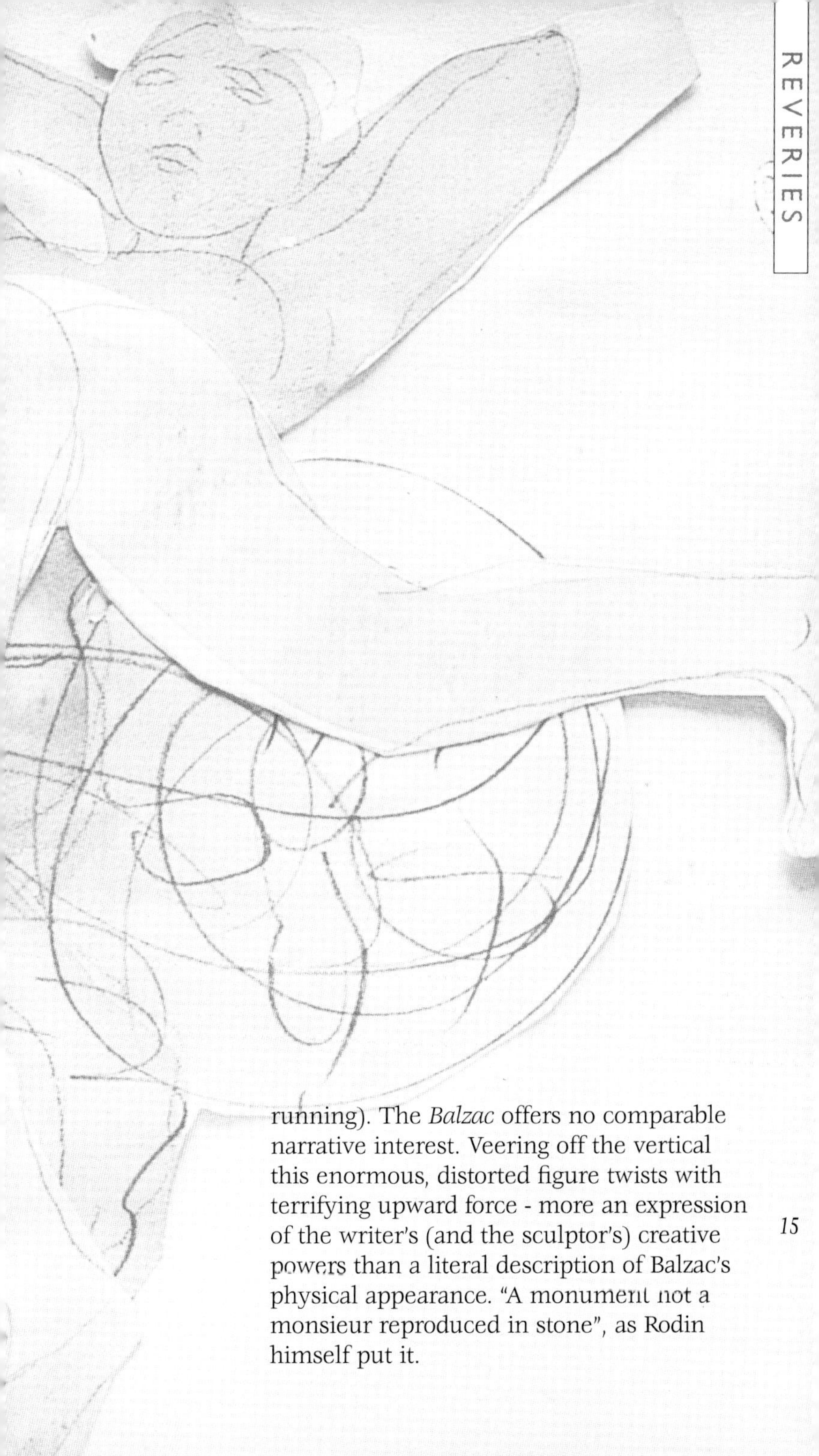

running). The *Balzac* offers no comparable narrative interest. Veering off the vertical this enormous, distorted figure twists with terrifying upward force - more an expression of the writer's (and the sculptor's) creative powers than a literal description of Balzac's physical appearance. "A monument not a monsieur reproduced in stone", as Rodin himself put it.

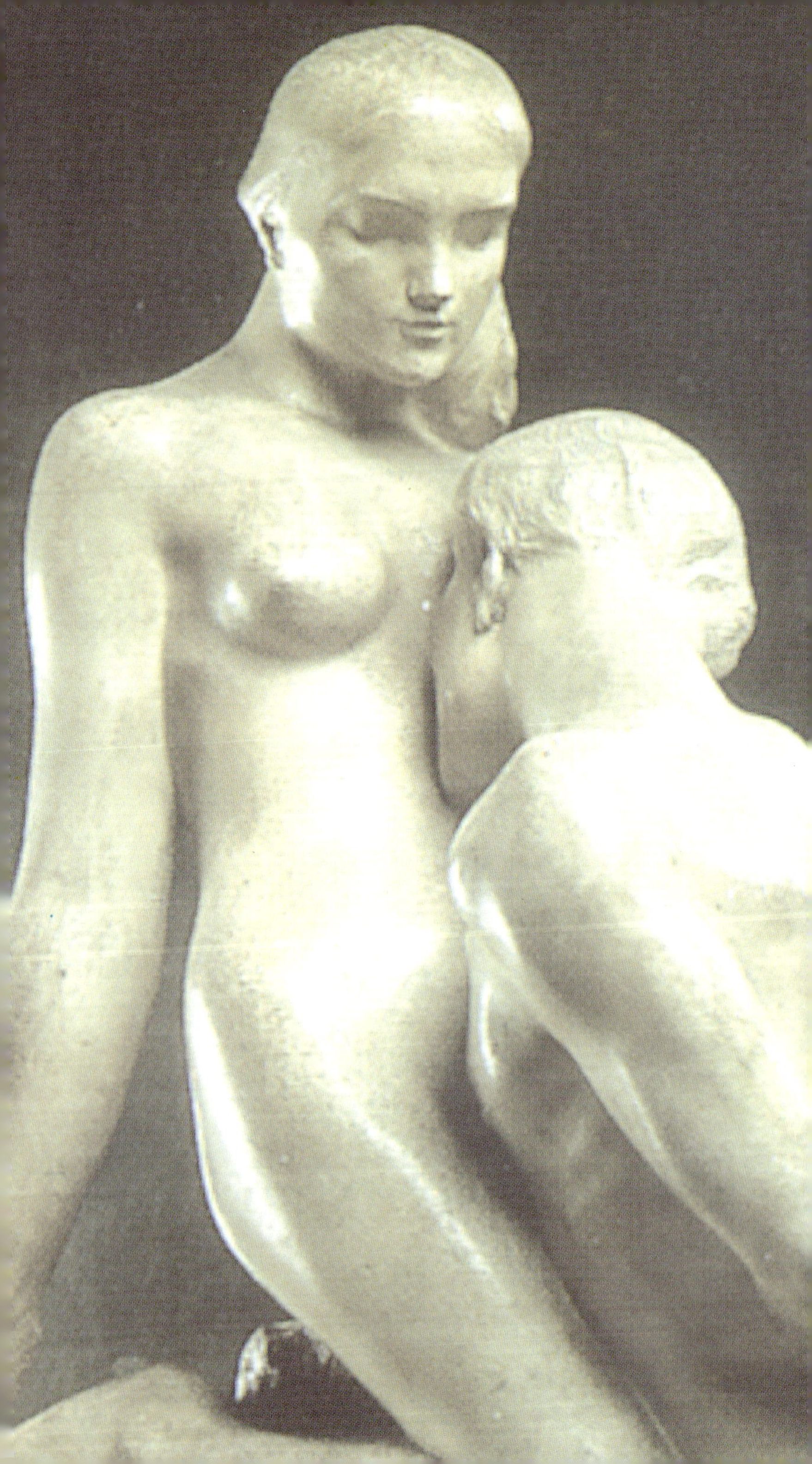

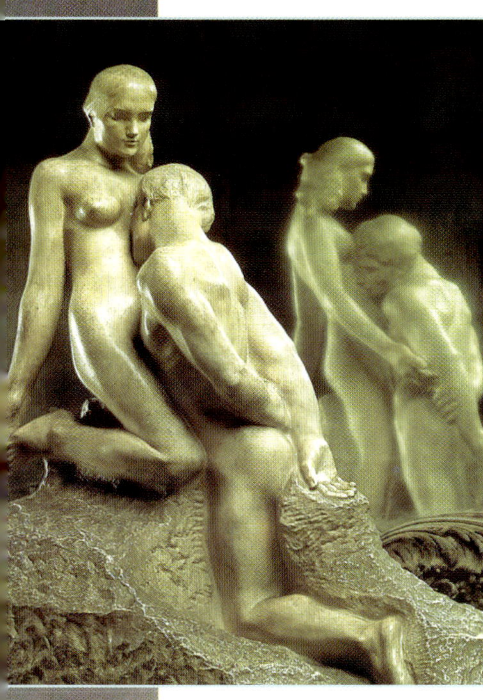

7 Eternal idol, 1889, plaster, Musée Rodin, Paris

However there is much that the works share. Both have been the subject of scandal and violent disapproval. A slightly earlier version of *The Kiss* was removed from an exhibition in Chicago in 1893 because the frank nature of the couple's embrace was considered too candid a sexual prelude for public taste to accept. Even as late as 1952 there was strong opposition to the Tate Gallery in London buying a copy for permanent display. The *Balzac* was rejected by the committee who had commissioned it, describing Rodin's monolith as "a shapeless mass, a nameless thing, a colossal foetus." Others at the time called it "a toad in a sack". The novelist Emile Zola and a number of other prominent public figures supported Rodin and petitioned the Parisian authorities to buy it for the city, to no avail. The controversy was then caught up in the explosive political storm then dividing French society: the Dreyfus affair, in which the State stood accused of complicity in anti-Semitic discrimination against a Jewish officer serving in the French army. Those who maintained that the government had acted dishonourably supported Rodin and the two issues were linked in the press.

What was probably considered most shocking about the statue was more rarely acknowledged. In a preparatory nude study for the piece, which was subsequently cast in bronze as an independent work, Rodin modelled a figure with his hands held together clasping his erect penis. The final *Balzac* is clothed - draped with a dressing gown that seems to seethe with seismic force. (Balzac, when he wrote, worked sixteen hours a day, ingested vast amounts of tobacco smoke and coffee and wore a dressing gown). But beneath its folds, a prominent bulge suggests strongly that this Balzac seems to be doing exactly the same as his predecessor. Moreover the form of the whole is distinctly phallic.

Both sculptures then share, at their heart, a dominant sexual motive power. This force is essential to much of Rodin's art and is mirrored in many of the stories recorded about the man himself. These concentrate on his physical pres-

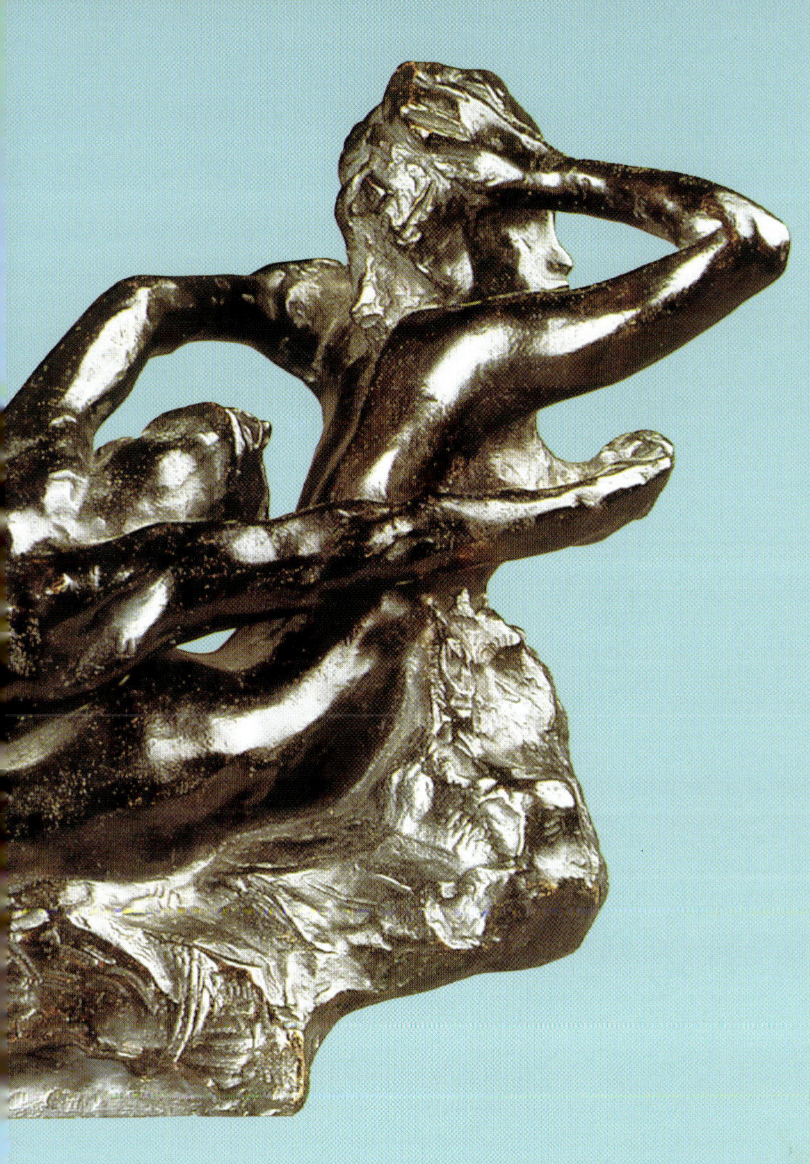

8 Fugit Amor, circa 1890, bronze, Musée Rodin, Paris

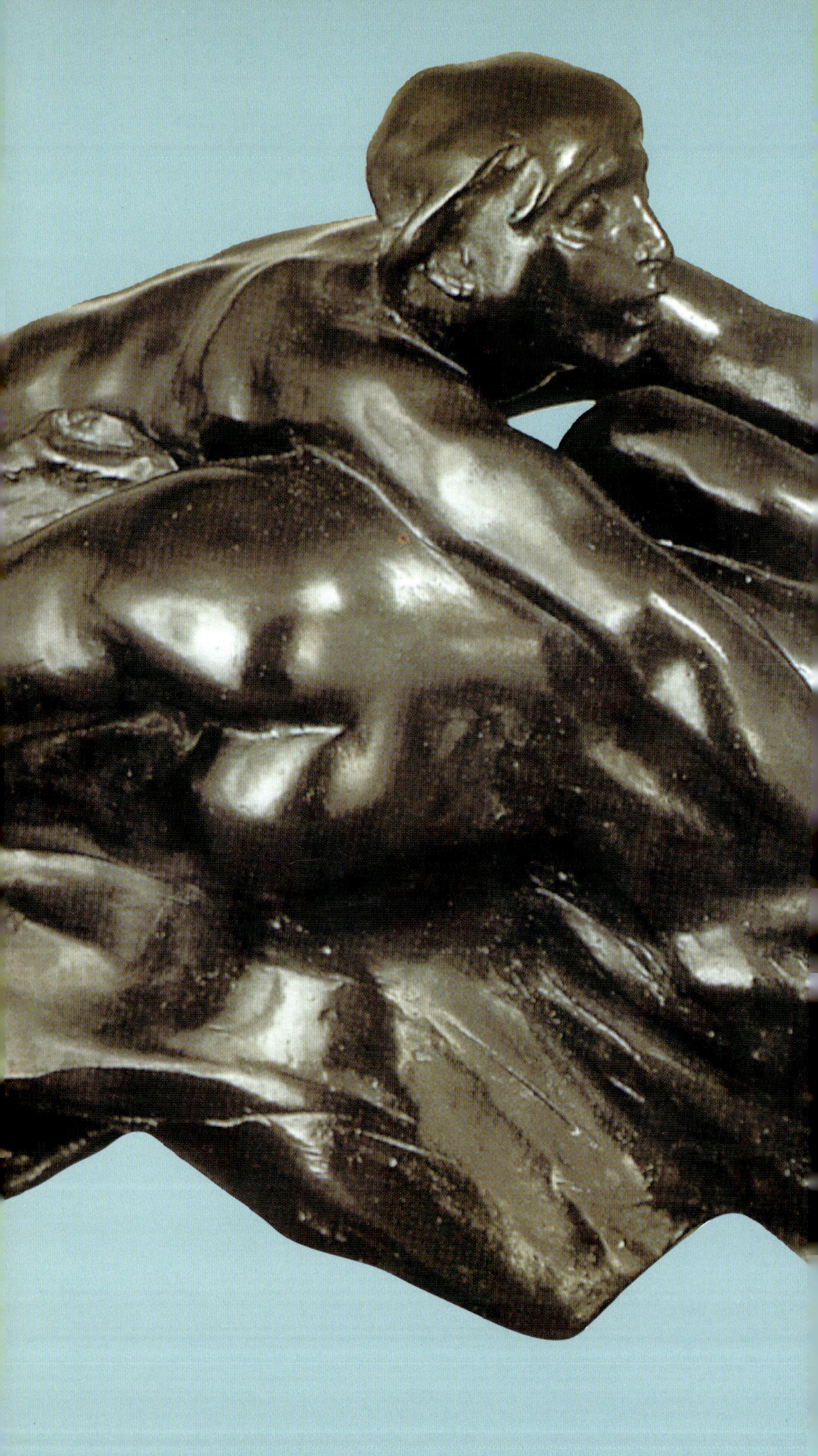

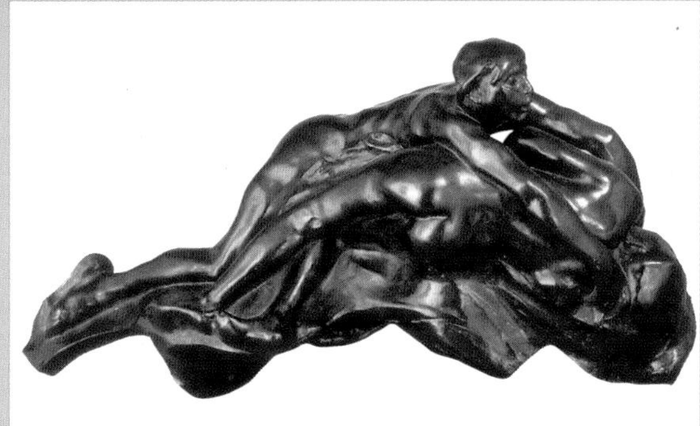

ence (despite or because of his small stature), his sexual energy, his hands, his piercing blue eyes, his heavy step. The American dancer Isadora Duncan, for example, describes how she invited the great sculptor to her studio in the early years of this century, where she performed one of her dances for him (he was in his sixties, she in her twenties) : "He began to knead my whole body as if it were clay, while from him emanated heat that scorched and melted me. My whole desire was to yield to him my entire being, and indeed I would have done so if it had not been that my absurd upbringing caused me to become frightened and I withdrew and sent him away bewildered . . . What a pity! How often I have regretted this childish miscomprehension which lost to me the divine chance of giving my virginity to the Great God Pan himself, the mighty Rodin." The prolific French diarist Edmond de Goncourt likened Rodin to a libidinous faun and recounted how at dinner with Monet and the painter's four daughters, Rodin had looked at each of them so directly that out

9 Paolo and Francesca, 1887, bronze, Musée Rodin, Paris

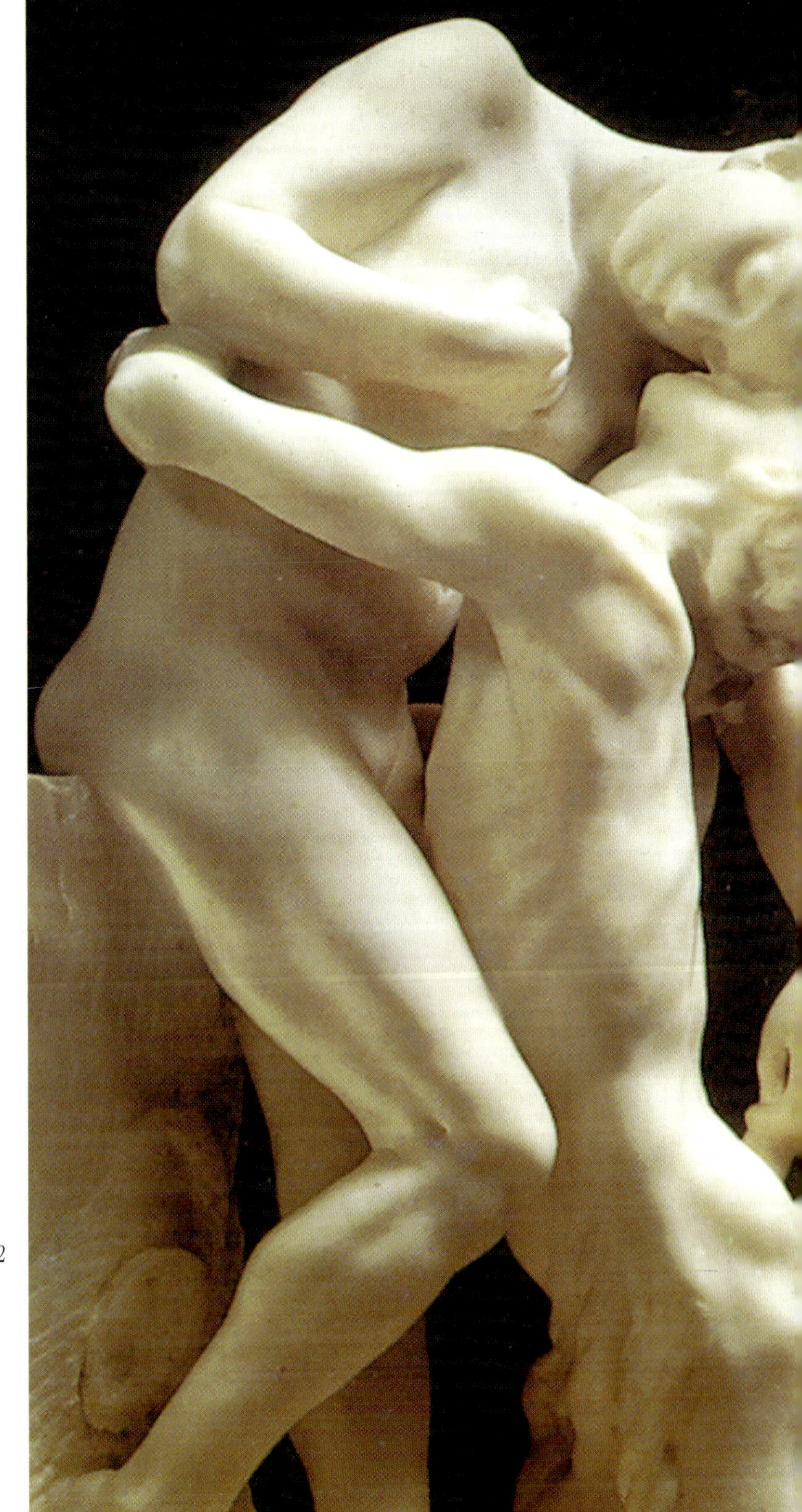

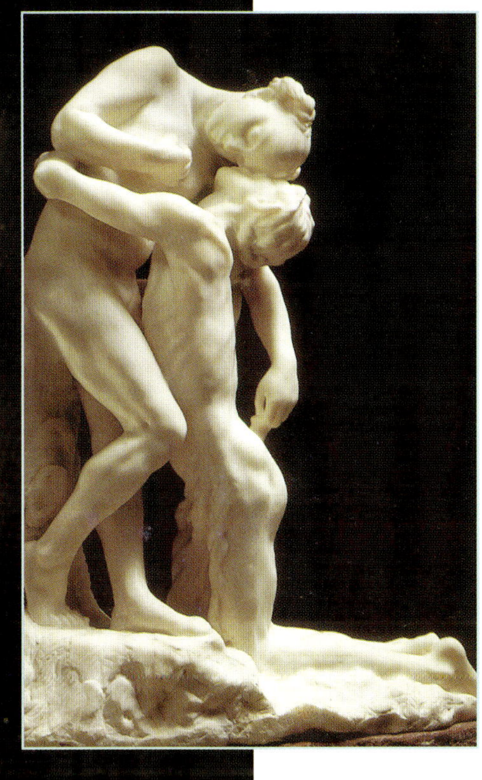

10 Vertumnus and Pommona, 1905, marble, Musée Rodin, Paris

of embarrassment one by one they left the table. Another anecdote tells of Rodin reverentially kissing the stomach of a female model posed for him in his Paris studio (which is exactly what Pygmalion is doing to Galatea in Rodin's sculpted version of this myth); the English playwright George Bernard Shaw relates how Rodin would take a huge draught of water in his mouth and spit it out onto the clay to keep it moist. The German writer Stefan Zweig describes Rodin at work in his old age (none of these stories, incidentally, concerns Rodin's younger years): "Then he no longer spoke. He would step forward, then retreat,

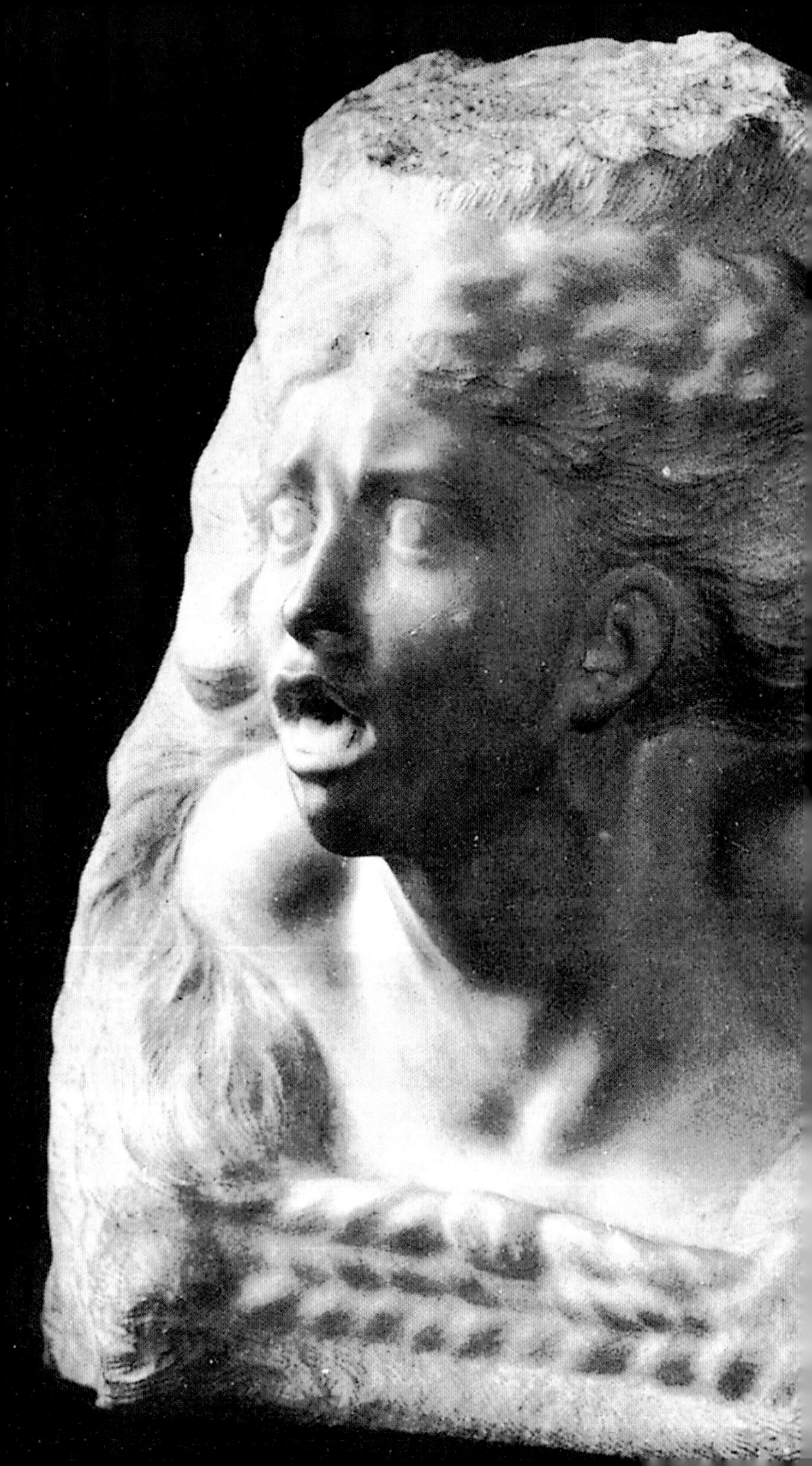

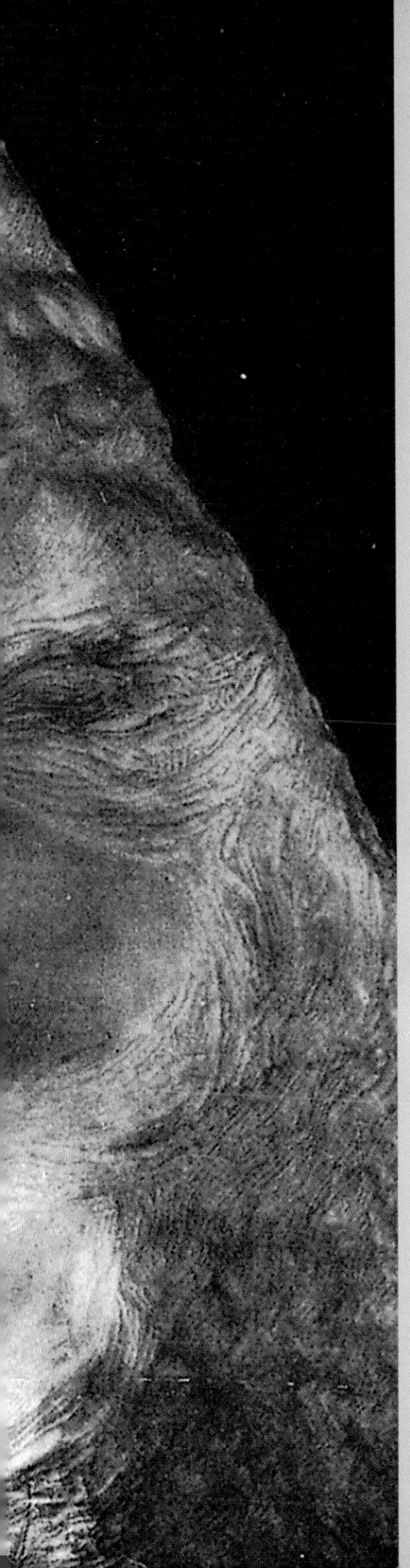

look at the figure in a mirror, mutter and utter unintelligible sounds, make changes and corrections. His eyes, which at table had been amiably attentive, now flashed with strange lights, and he seemed to have grown larger and younger. He worked, worked, and worked with the entire passion and force of his heavy body; whenever he stepped forward or back the floor creaked."

It is such physical, sensual and on occasion overtly sexual details as these which impressed themselves on his contemporaries. His sculptures have had a comparable effect on later viewers. The British sculptor Henry Moore, who never met Rodin,

11 The Tempest, marble

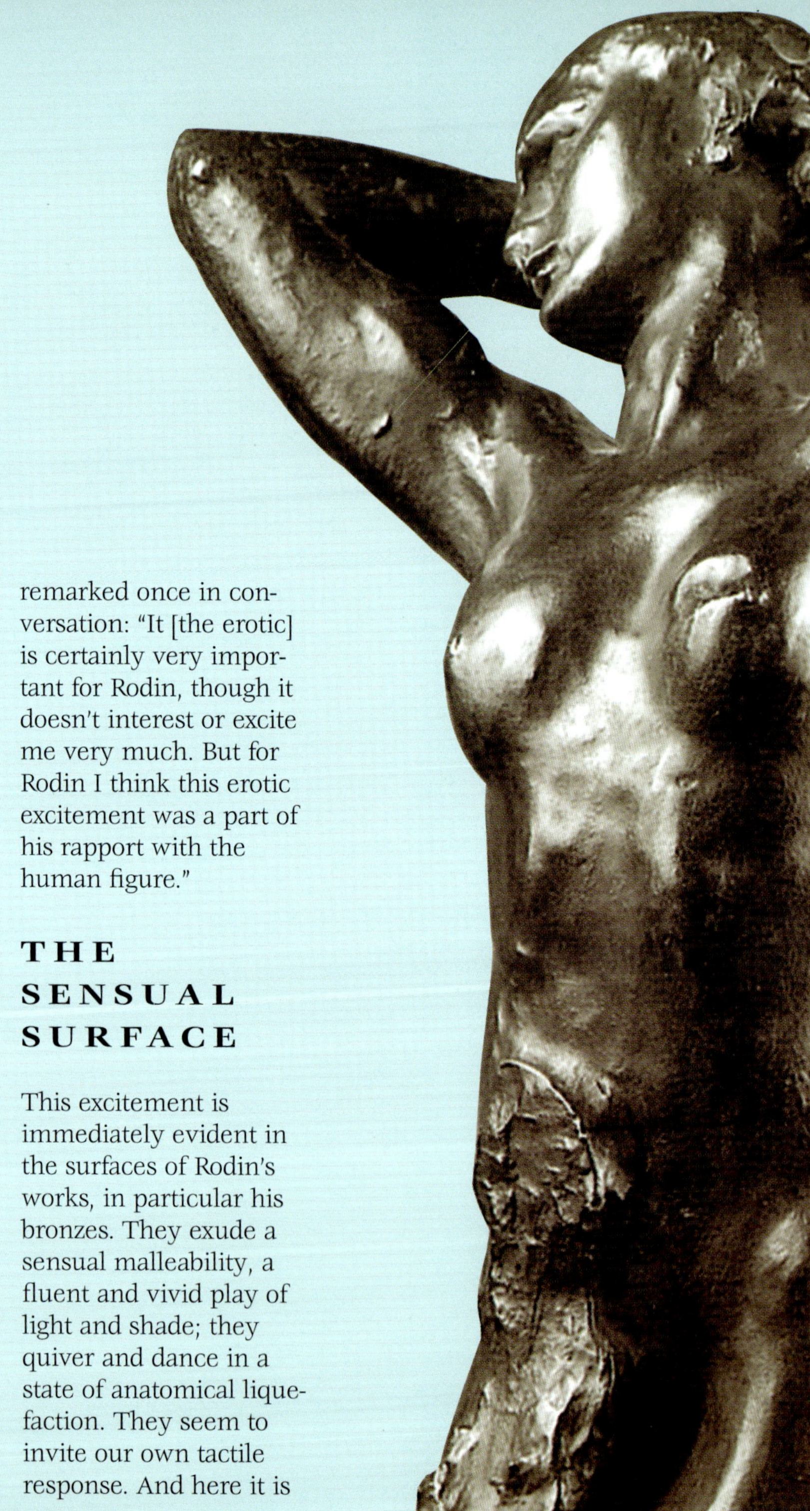

remarked once in conversation: "It [the erotic] is certainly very important for Rodin, though it doesn't interest or excite me very much. But for Rodin I think this erotic excitement was a part of his rapport with the human figure."

THE SENSUAL SURFACE

This excitement is immediately evident in the surfaces of Rodin's works, in particular his bronzes. They exude a sensual malleability, a fluent and vivid play of light and shade; they quiver and dance in a state of anatomical liquefaction. They seem to invite our own tactile response. And here it is

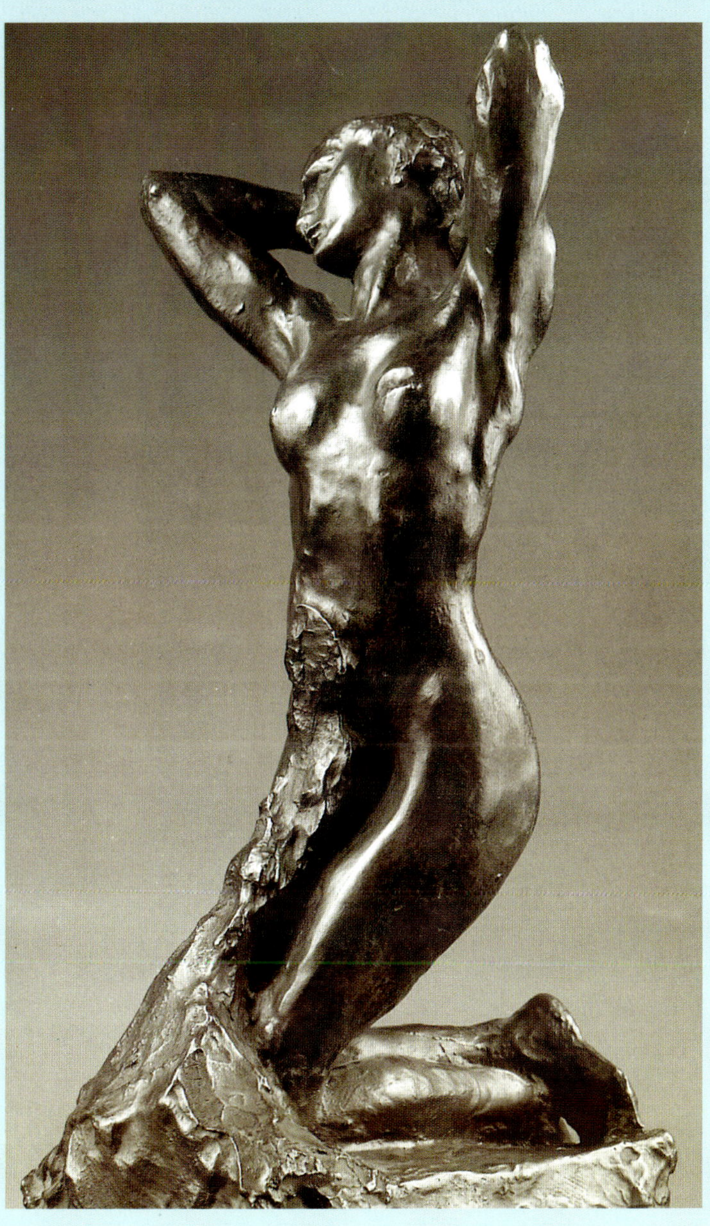

12 The Toilet of Venus, bronze, Musée Rodin, Paris.

worth recalling that Rodin worked primarily as a modeller. His marbles were largely speaking carved by assistants, copying bronze or plaster originals. Rodin himself very rarely cut or hacked or chiselled (*The Tempest* - 11; *Dawn* - 5). Instead, he pressed, rubbed, smoothed, caressed and moulded wet clay with his hands. The clay figure would then be cast in either plaster or bronze. The process of working was, for him, inherently manual, digital, ductile and seductive. Works such as *Eternal Idol - 7, Vertumnus and Pomona - 10,* The *Toilet of Venus - 12, Torso of a Young Woman - 4* and *Eternal Spring - 19* (6-10) make manifest this

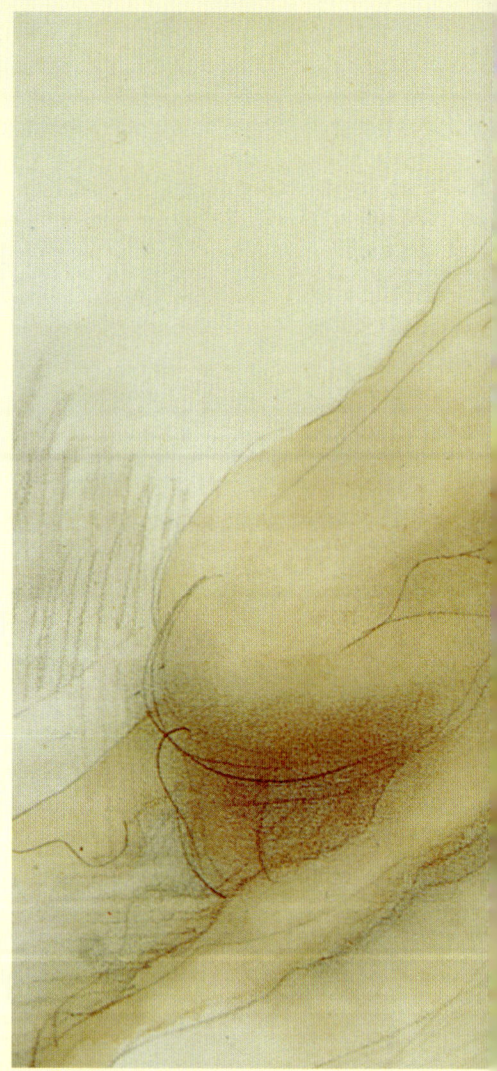

13 The Temple of love, lead and watercolour.

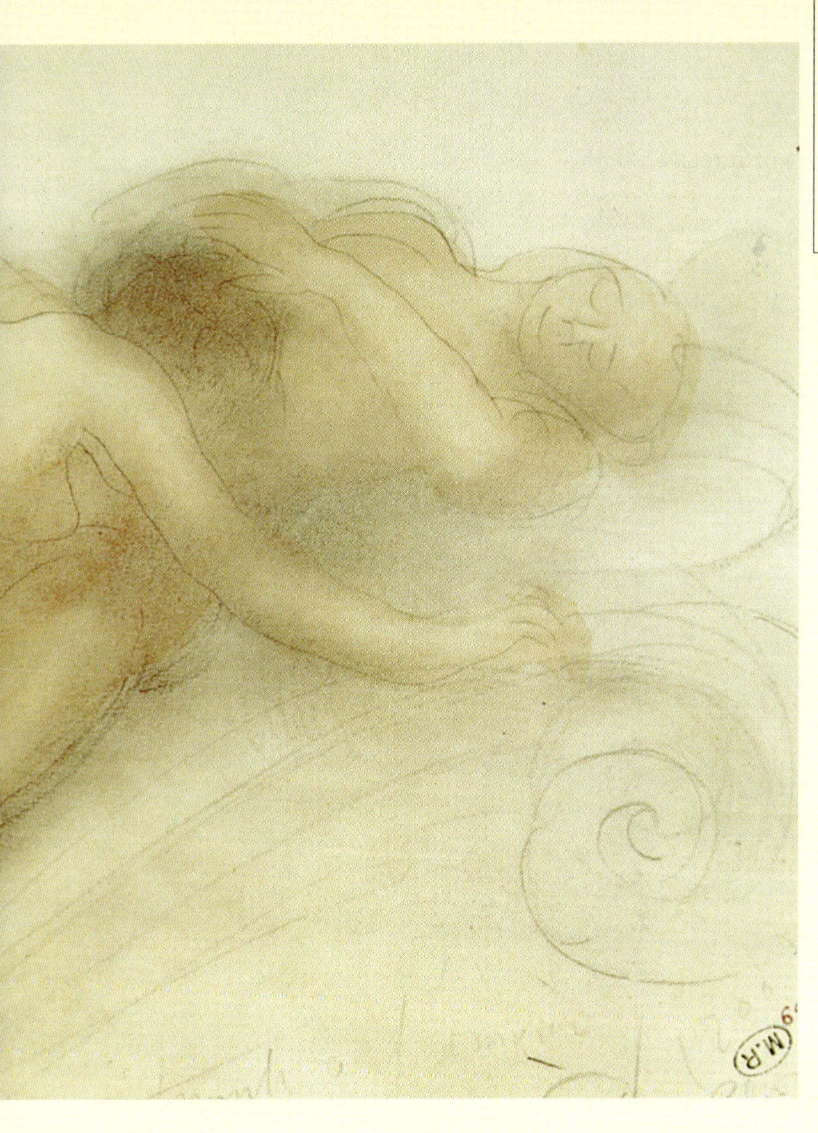

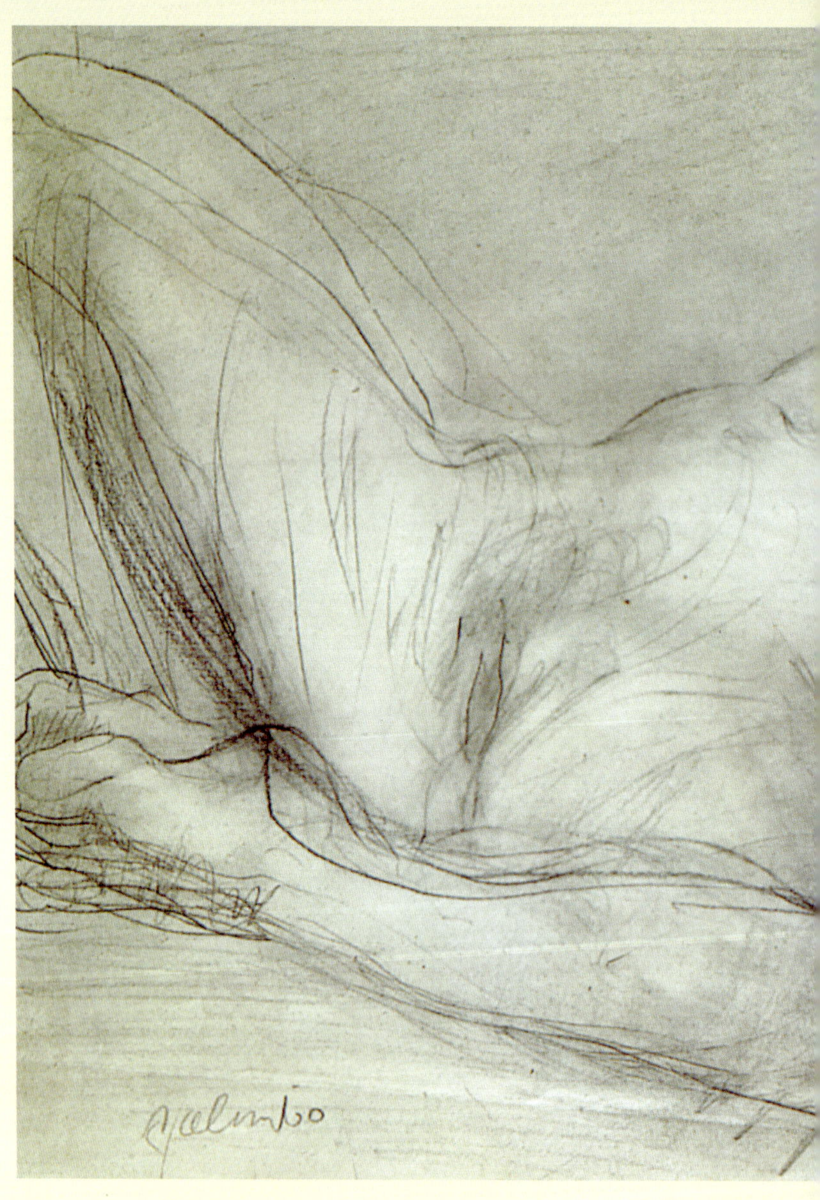

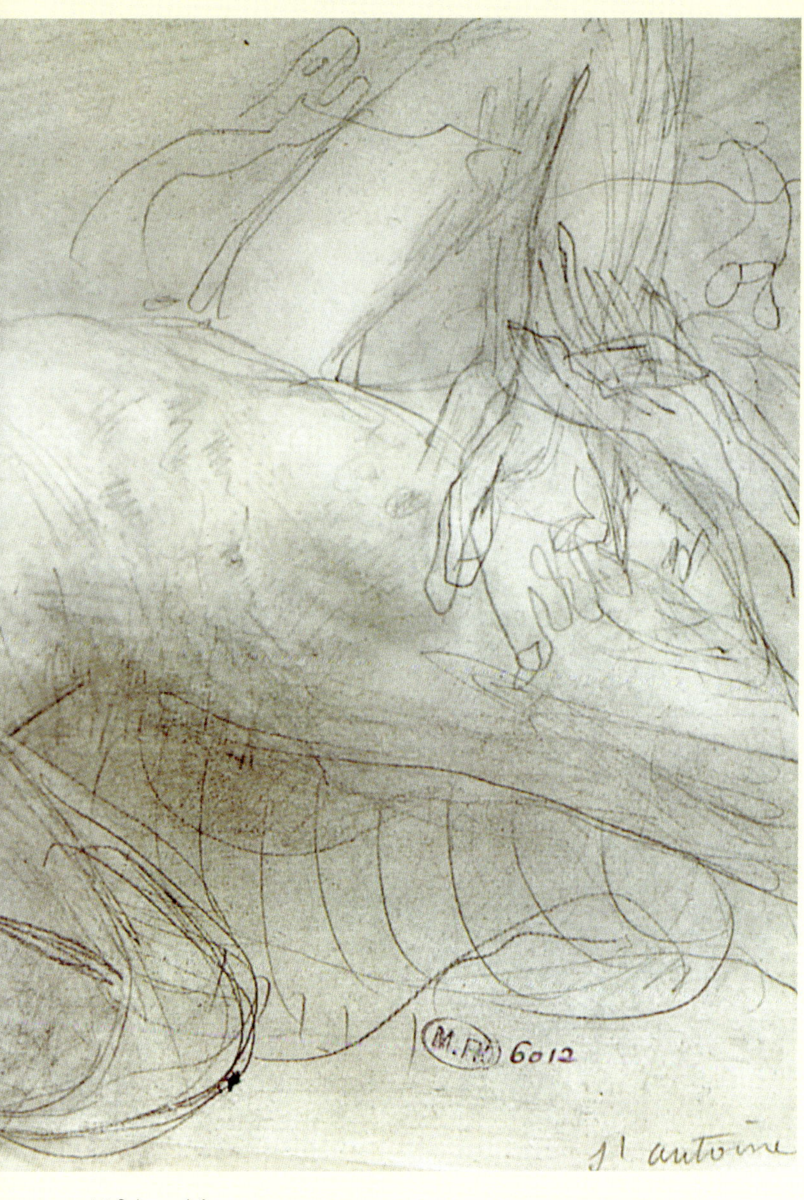

14 Salammbô

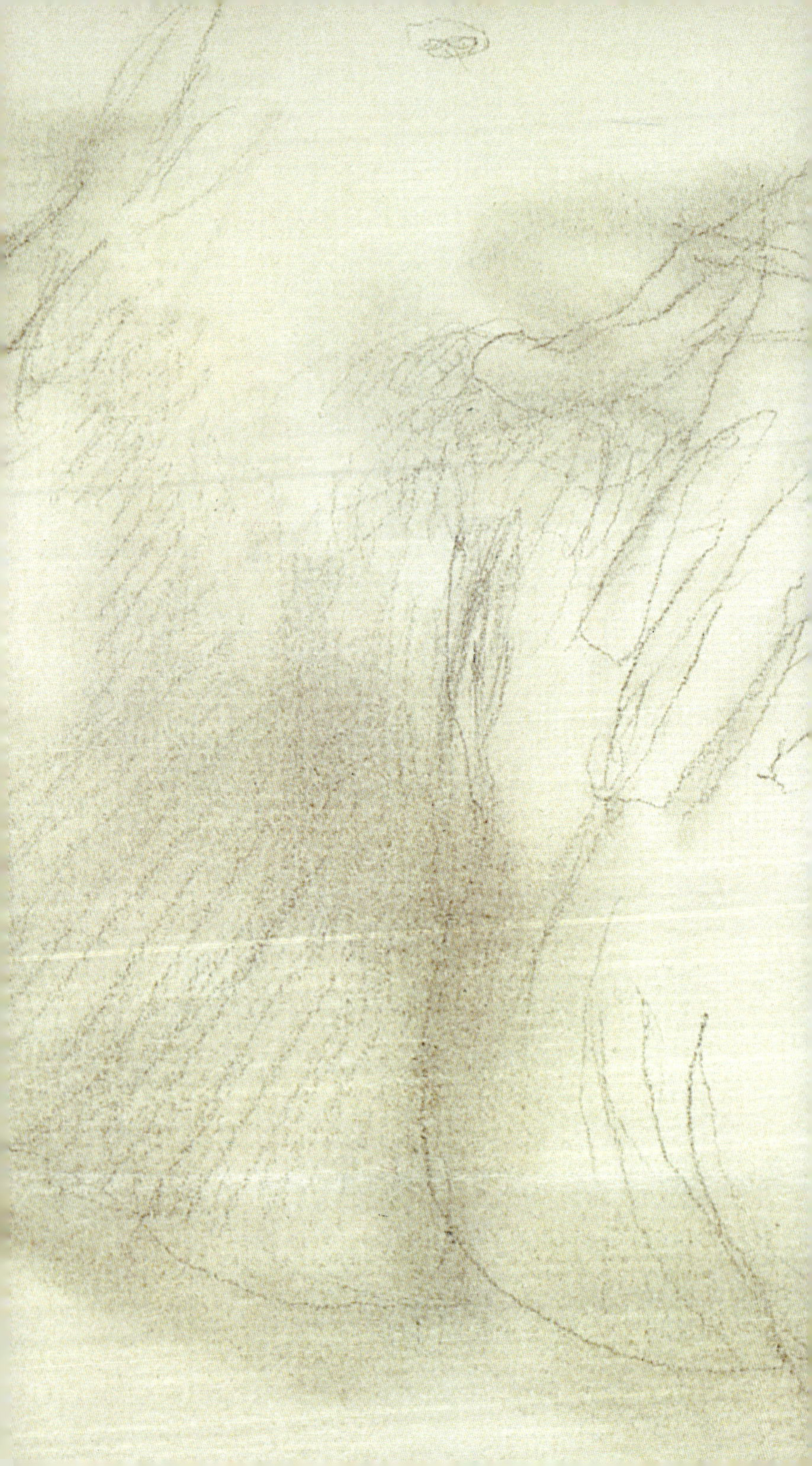

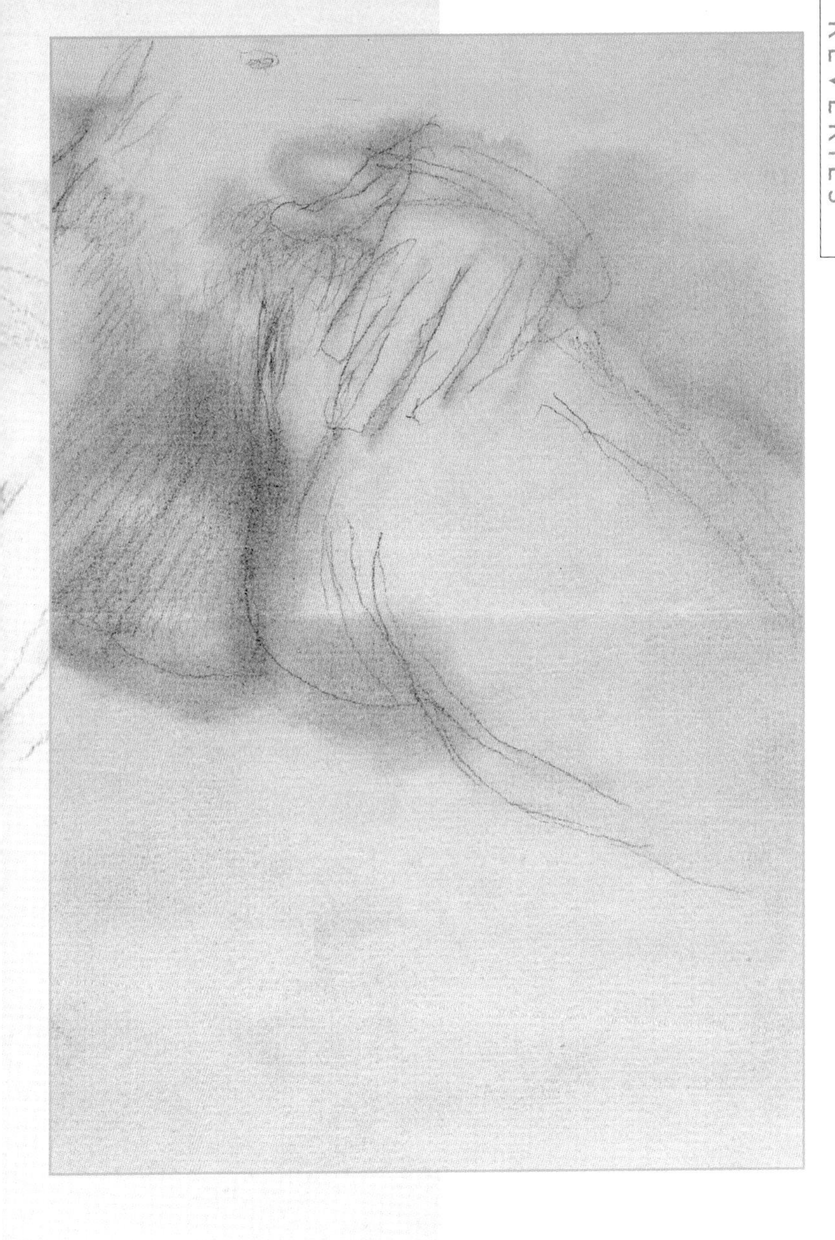

15 Hand on a woman's sex, lead and charcoal on paper

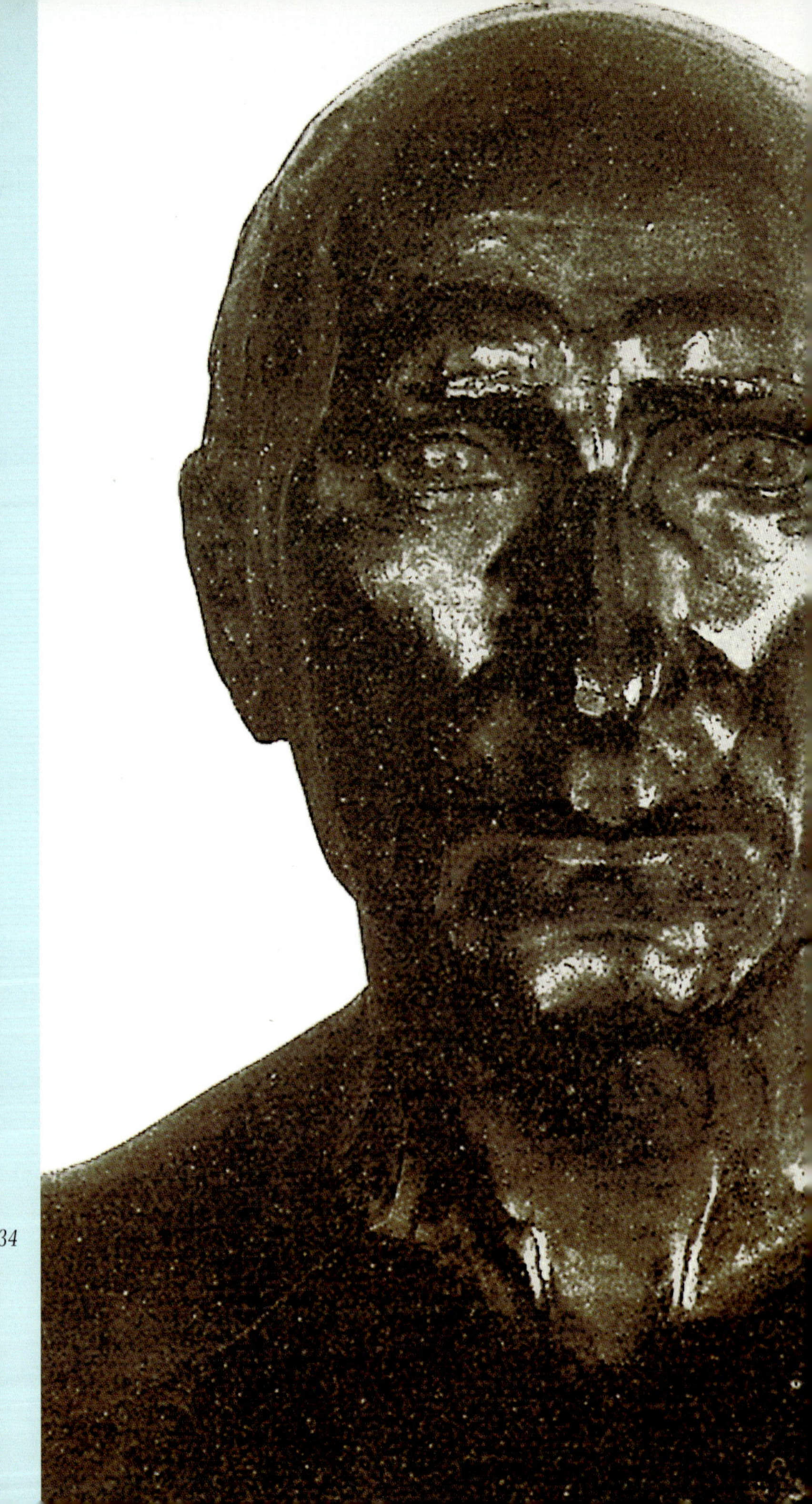

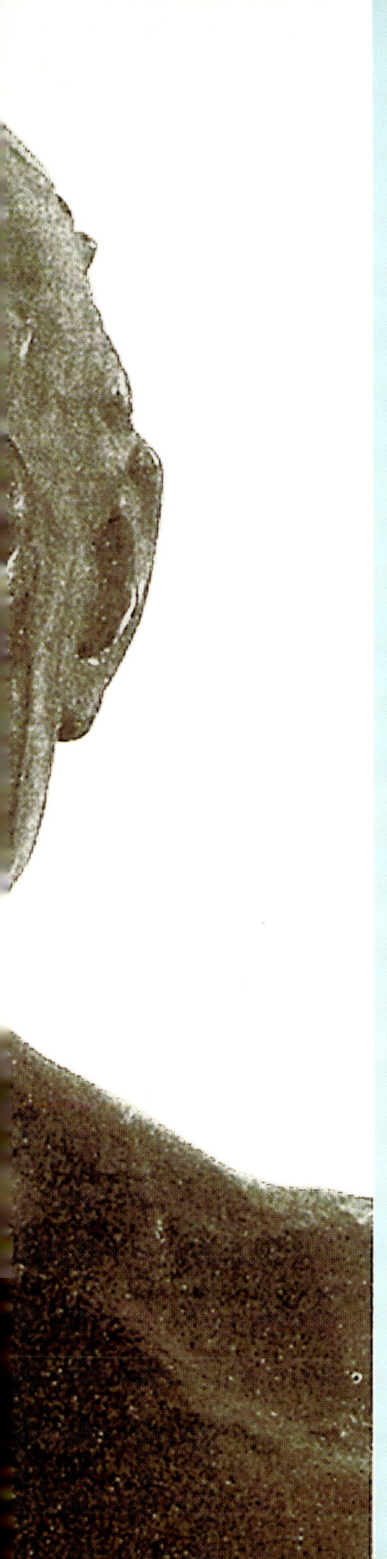

debt to an erotic muse both in the poses of the figures and the texture of the finish.

In the beginning none of this was quite so clear. Rodin's erotic liberation was to come later in his life. "I did not know that, distrusted at twenty they [women] would charm me at seventy. I distrusted them because I was timid", he is recorded as saying. In fact the details of Rodin's early life have a seriousness and austerity about them that would seem to exclude any erotic or sexual inspiration. Rodin was born (1840) into a poor, hard-working Parisian family. His father (16) disapproved of his son's desire to become a sculptor. Rodin was forced to study in his own time while he supported himself by producing pretty

16 Jean-Baptisite Rodin, father of the artist, circa 1864, bronze, Musée Rodin, Paris

rococo-style sculptures as an assistant in a large, commercial studio. As a young man he also spent a year in a religious institution as a novice after his sister died, although he never took orders.

Rodin's first romantic and sexual experiences had no direct effect on his earliest independent sculptures which share a robust virility both in style and subject - male nude figures and male portrait heads. During his twenties he met a young girl, called Rose Beuret, herself twenty years of age, in a sweet shop. She was a seamstress, they became lovers and in 1866 she bore him a son whom Rodin more or less completely ignored for the rest of his life. She and Rodin never separated; she was to die only a few months before him. And despite all the affairs and assignations that Rodin was to enjoy once he had lost his timidity (*Hélène de*

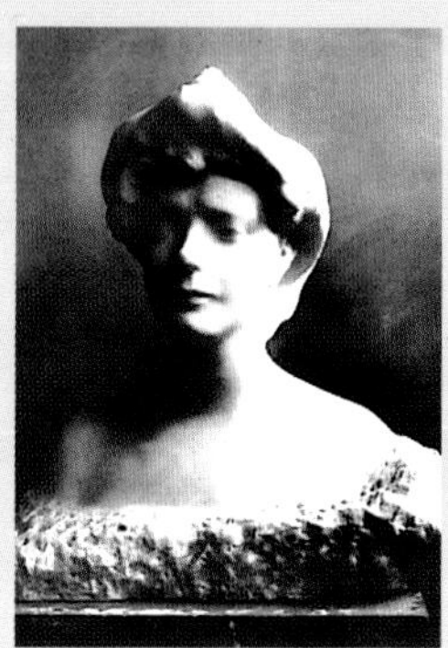

17 Hélène Nostitz, circa 1902

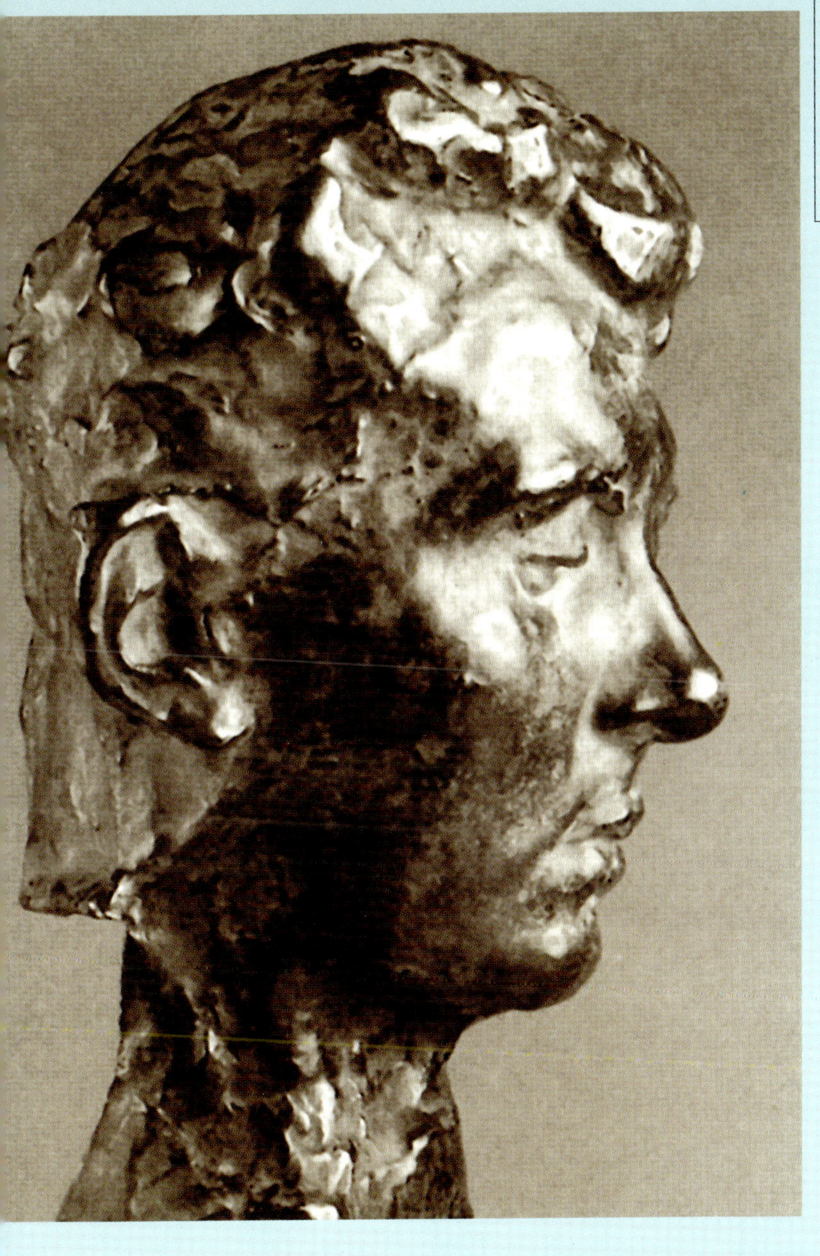

18 Rose Beuret, circa 1890, bronze, Musée Rodin, Paris

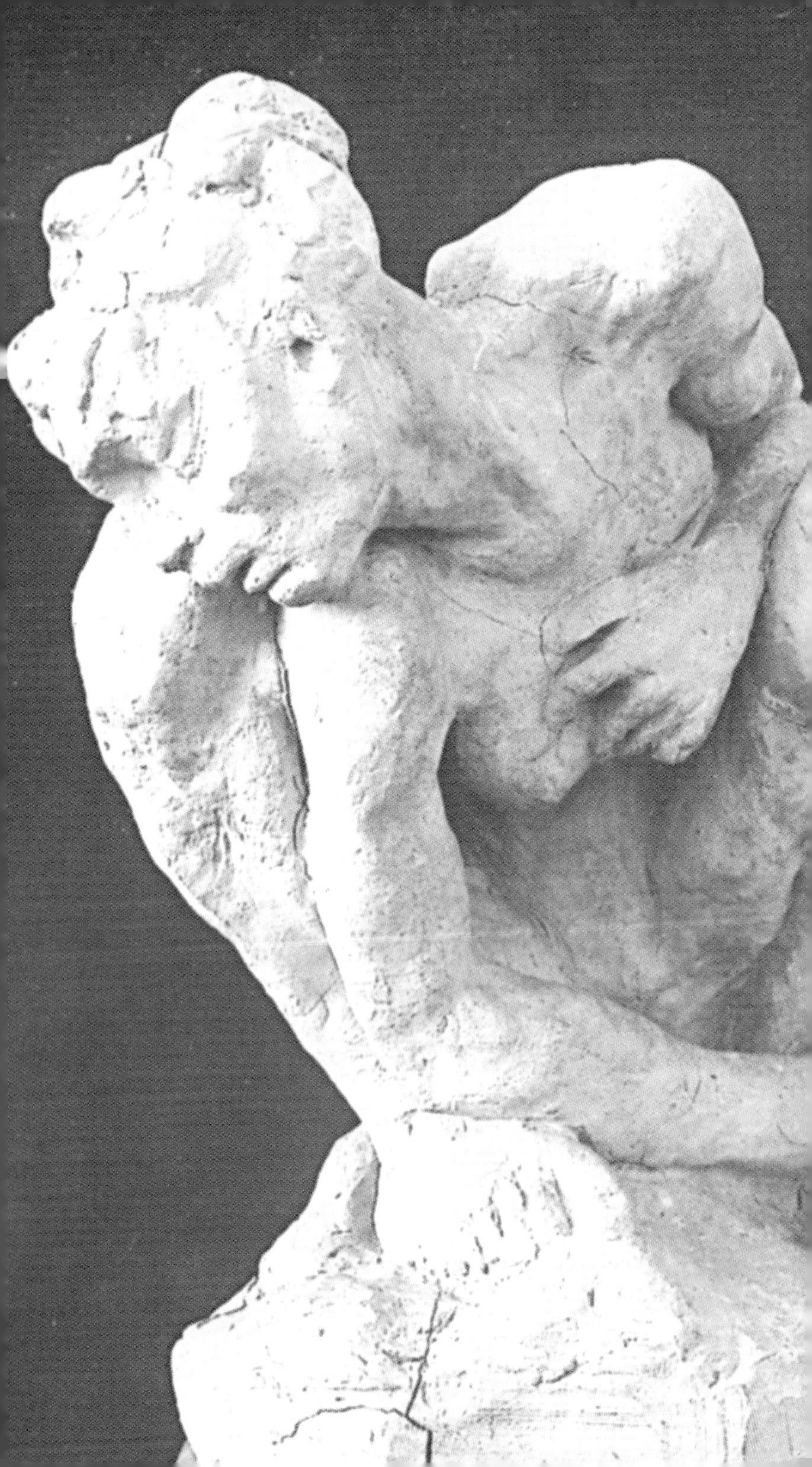

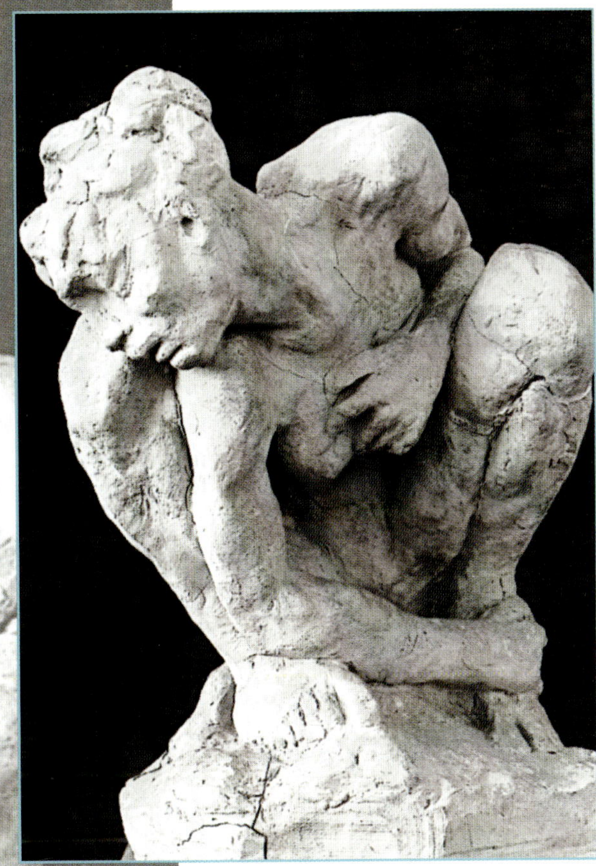

19 Eternal Spring, 1884, marble, Musée Rodin, Paris

Nostitz - 17), they finally married in 1917, both in their seventies, two weeks before she died. The words of a short note he wrote to her in 1913 speak of a loyalty and warmth that extended over fifty years: "My kind Rose, I send you this letter as a thought I am having about the greatness of this present God made me while putting you close to me. Put this in your generous heart. I will come back on Tuesday." Who knows whom he might have been with on Monday; but Rose never deserted him.

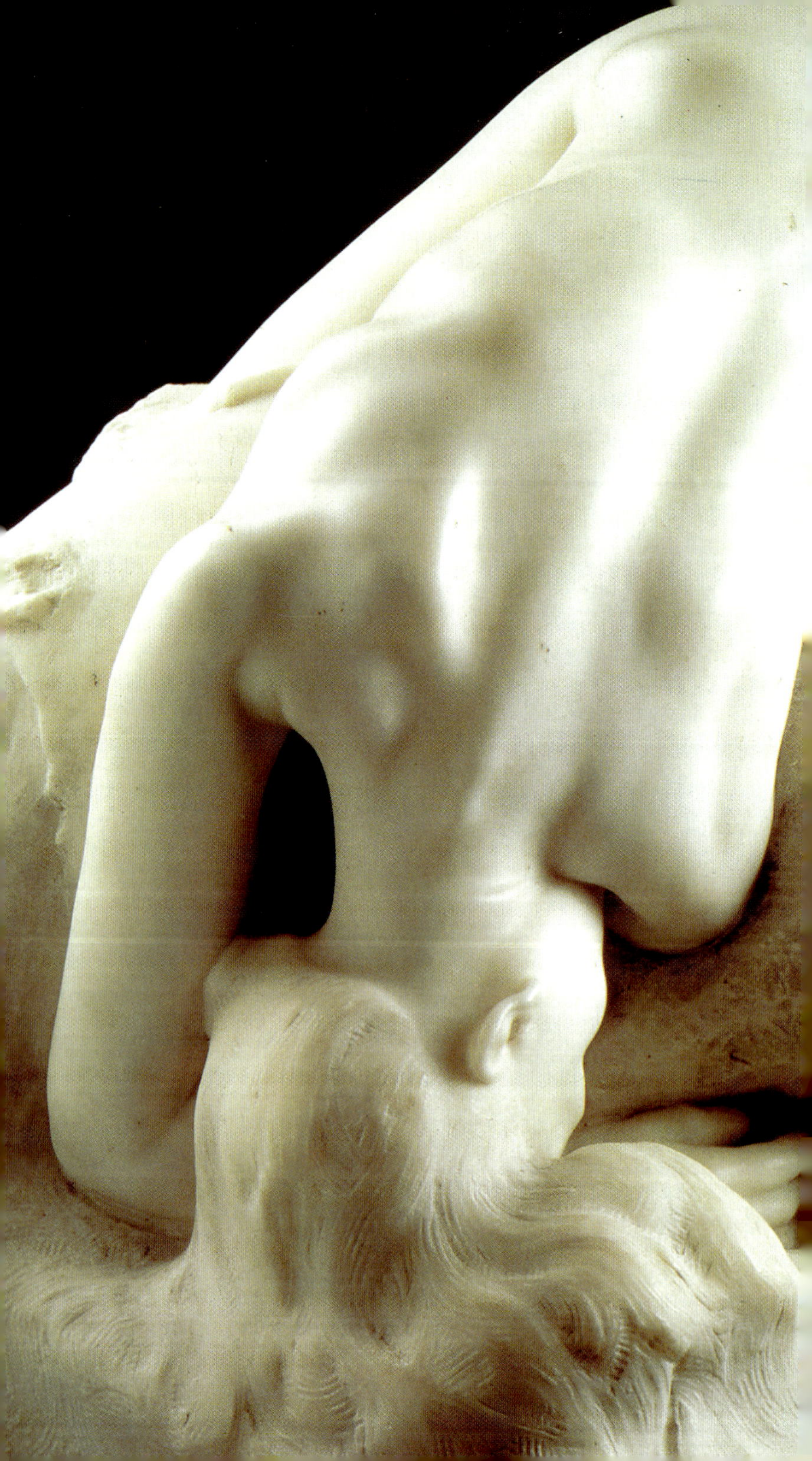

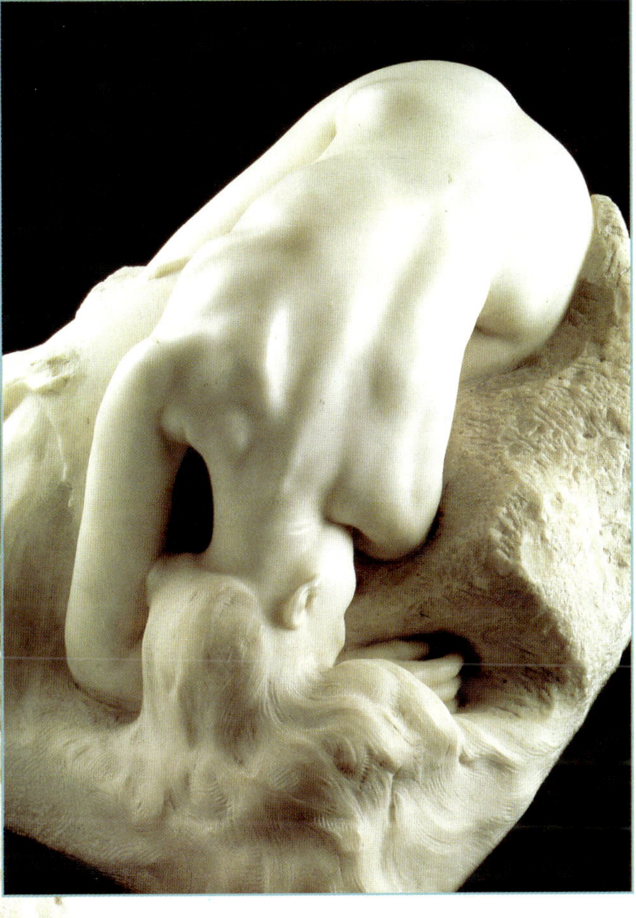

20 Danaid

Rose modelled for Rodin (18) but cannot properly be described as an erotic muse: this was a role to be filled by his other mistresses, one above all the others. Their early years together were in any case marked by poverty and hard-work. In addition, the outbreak of war with Prussia in 1870 forced the couple to leave for Belgium so that Rodin could find work to support them. They only returned to Paris in 1877.

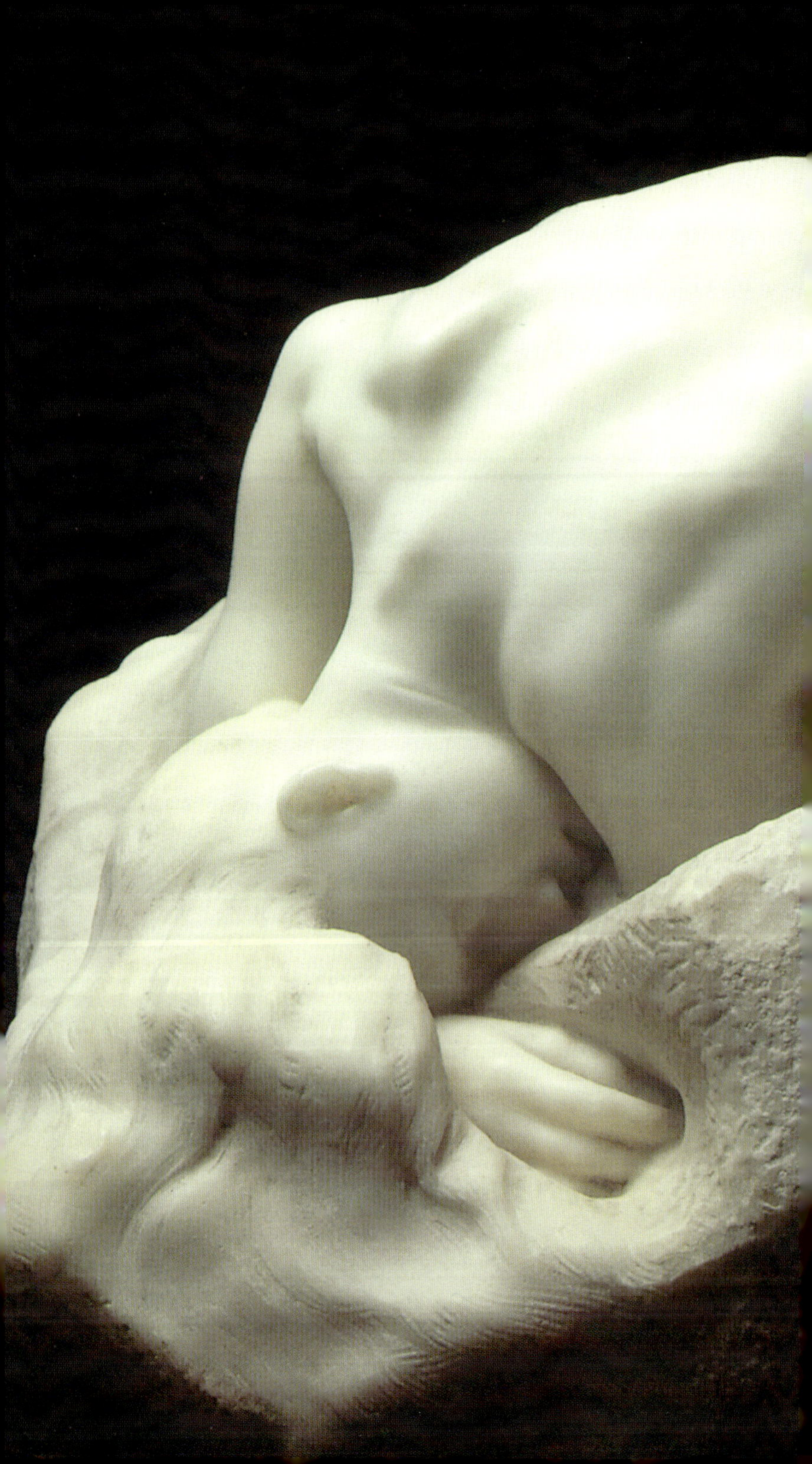

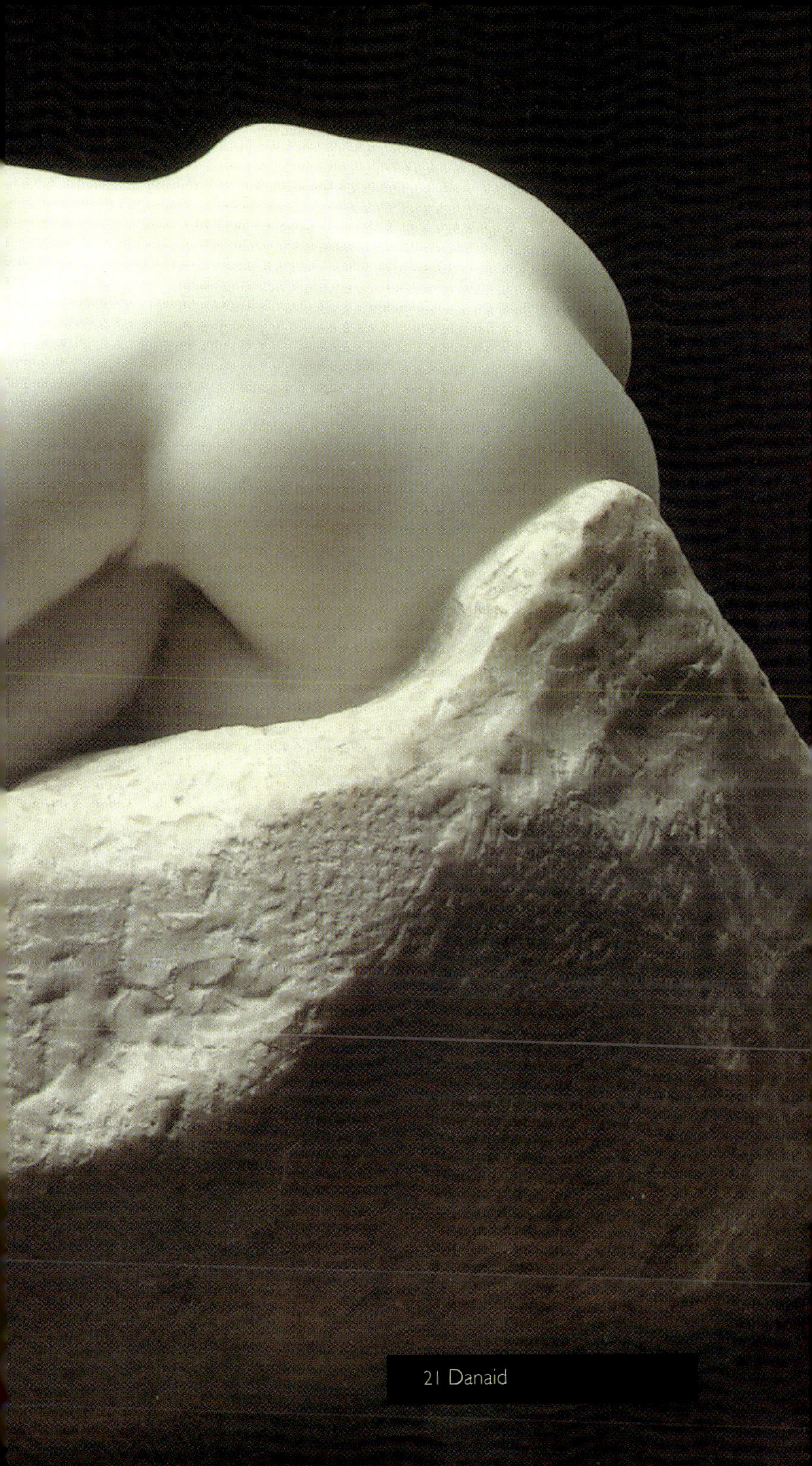
21 Danaid

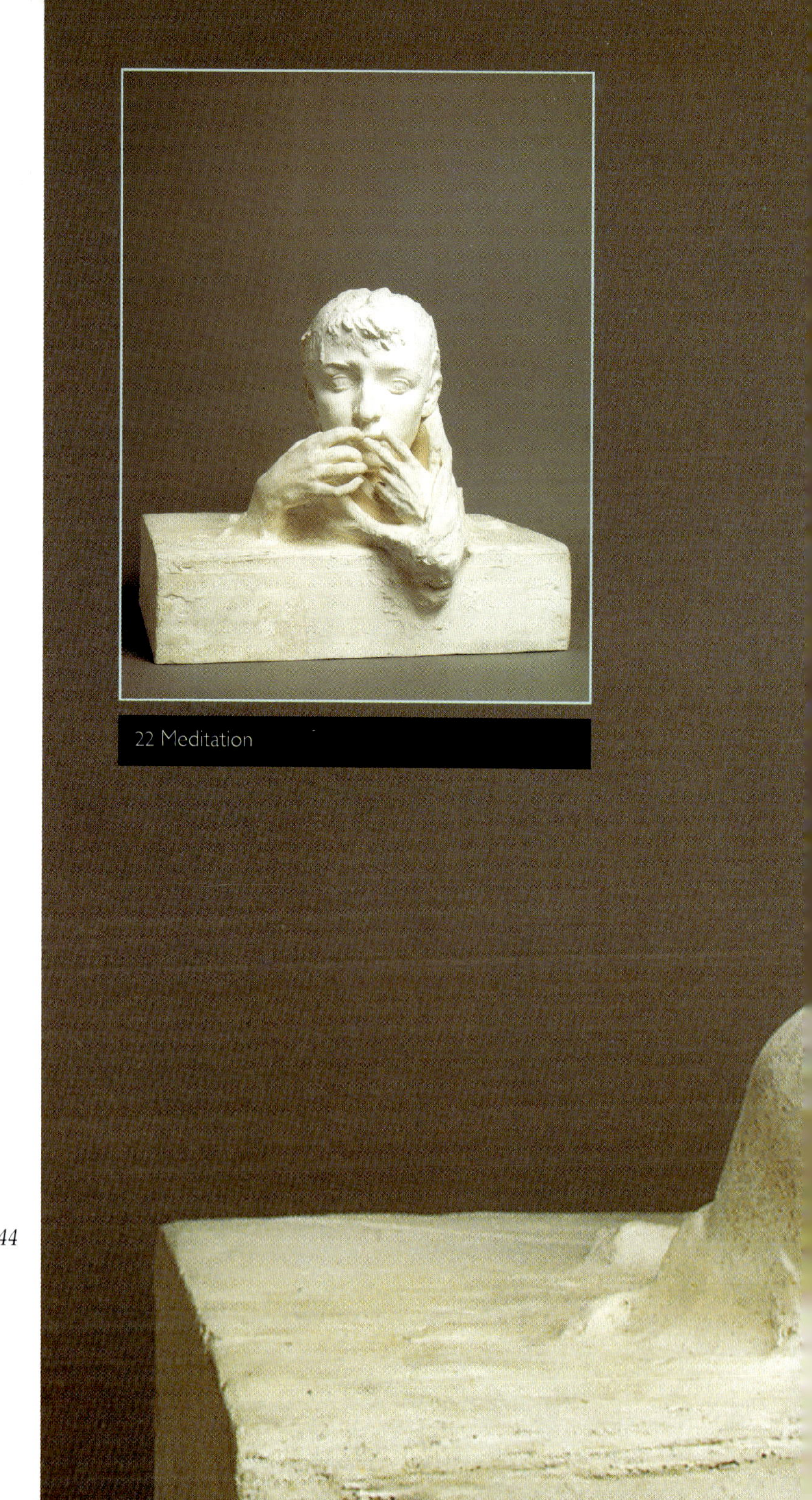

22 Meditation

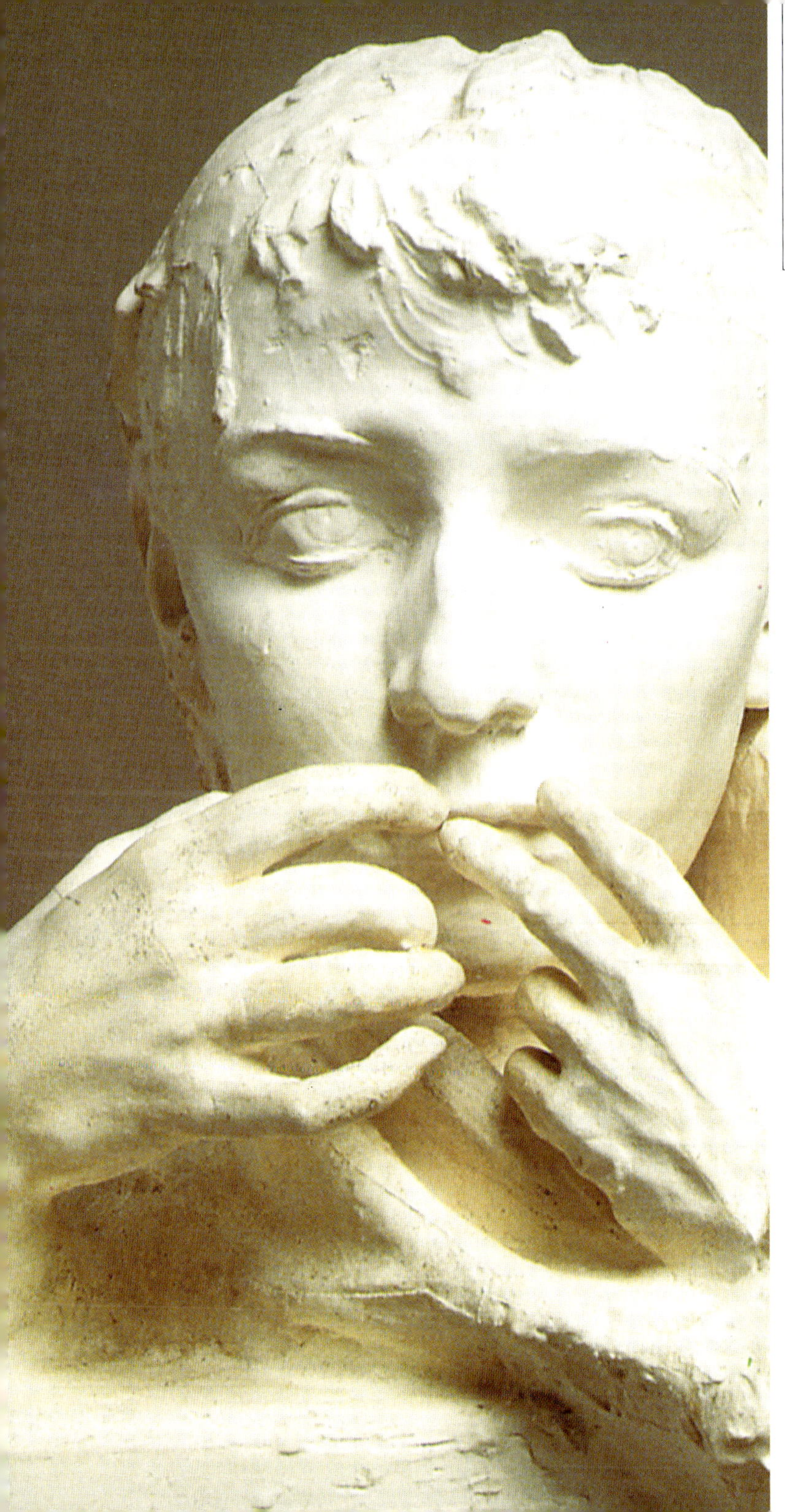

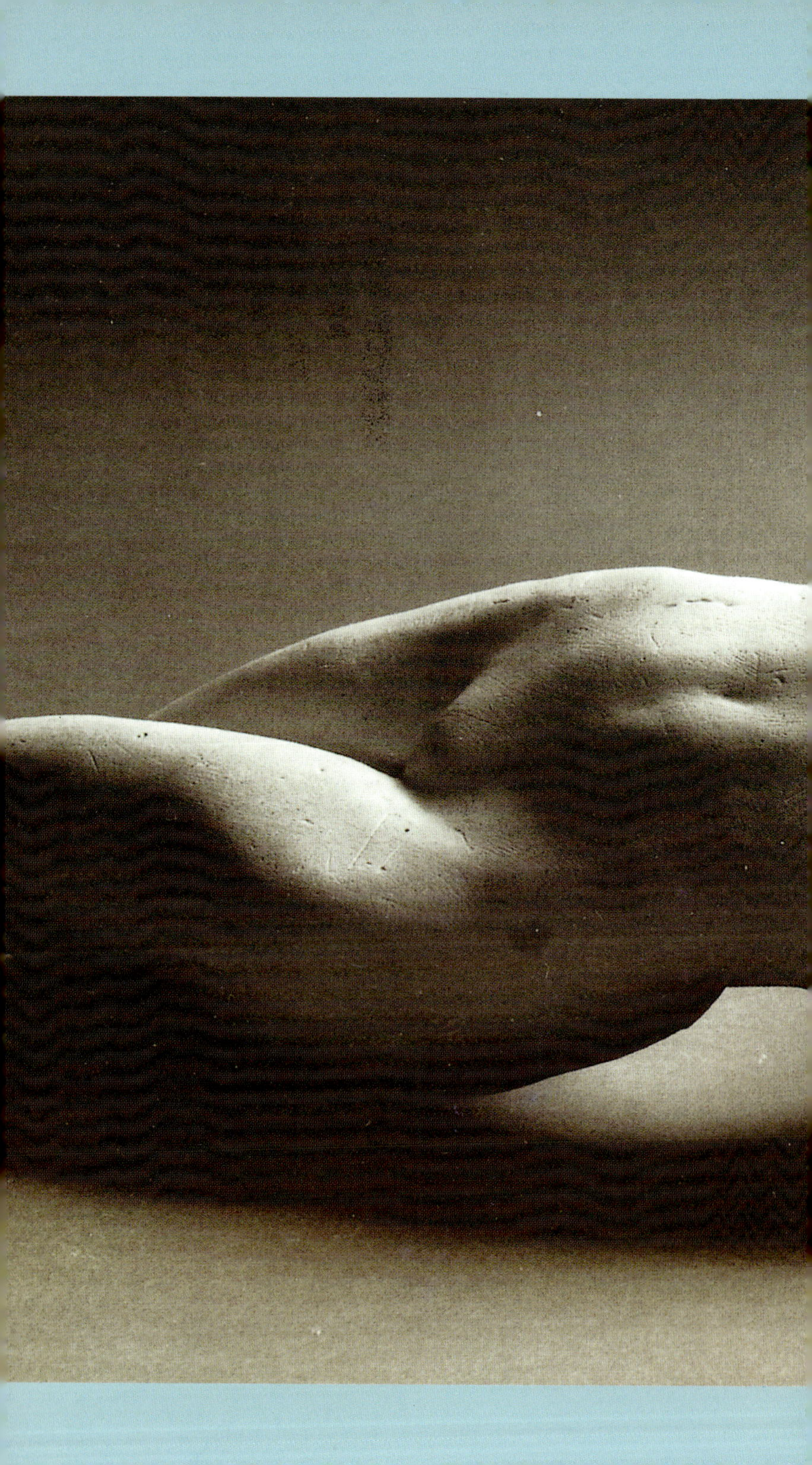

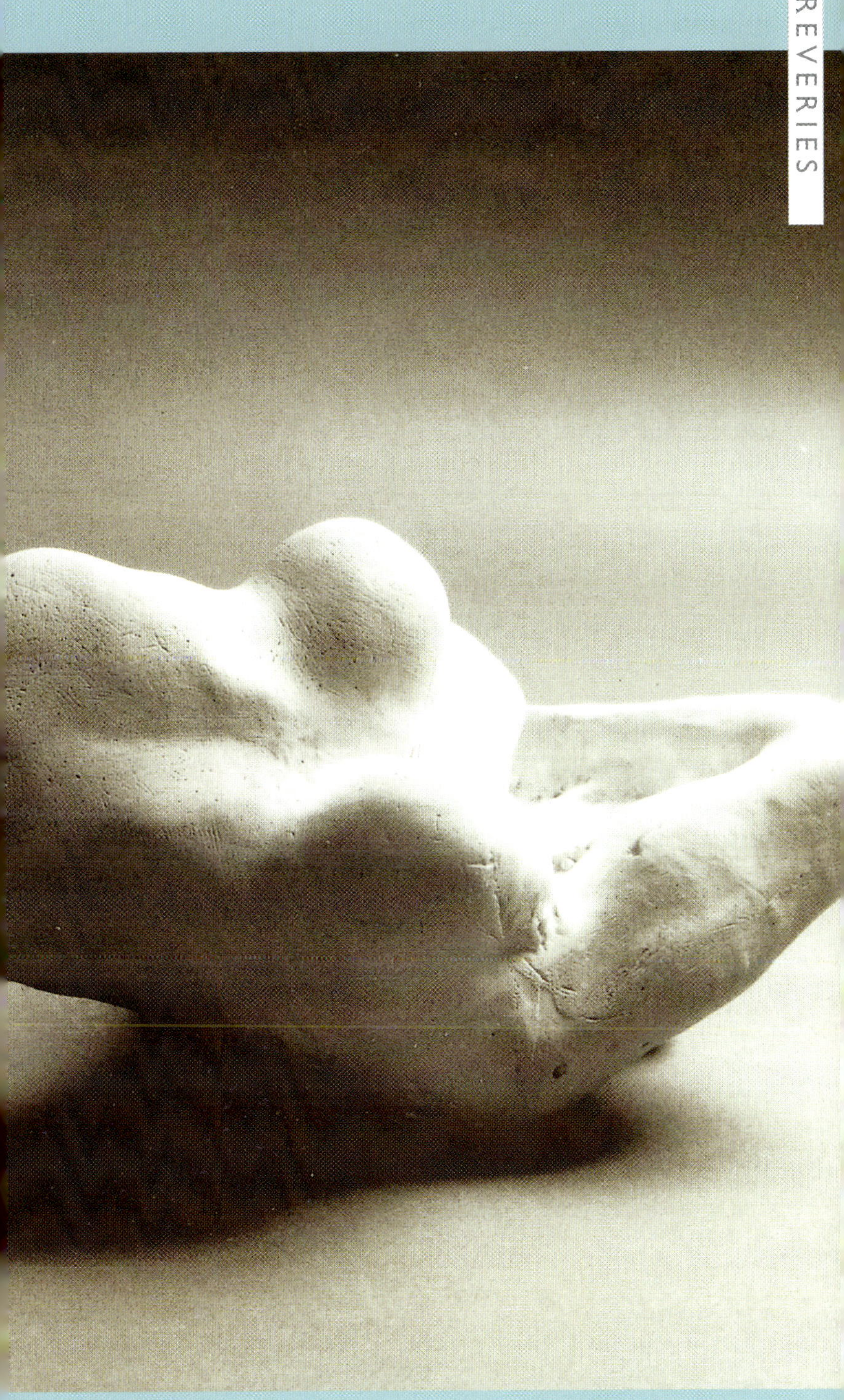

23 Torso of Adèle

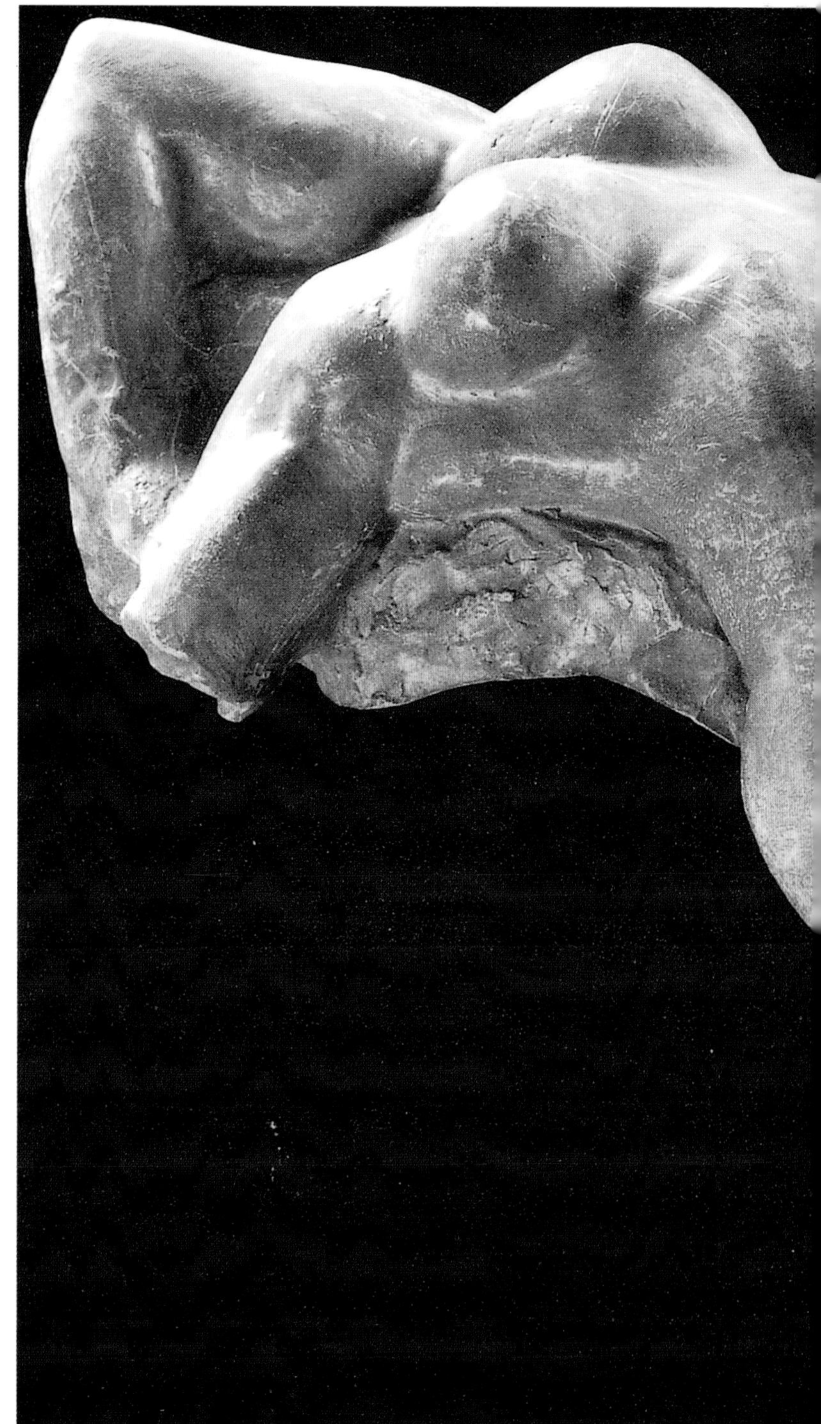

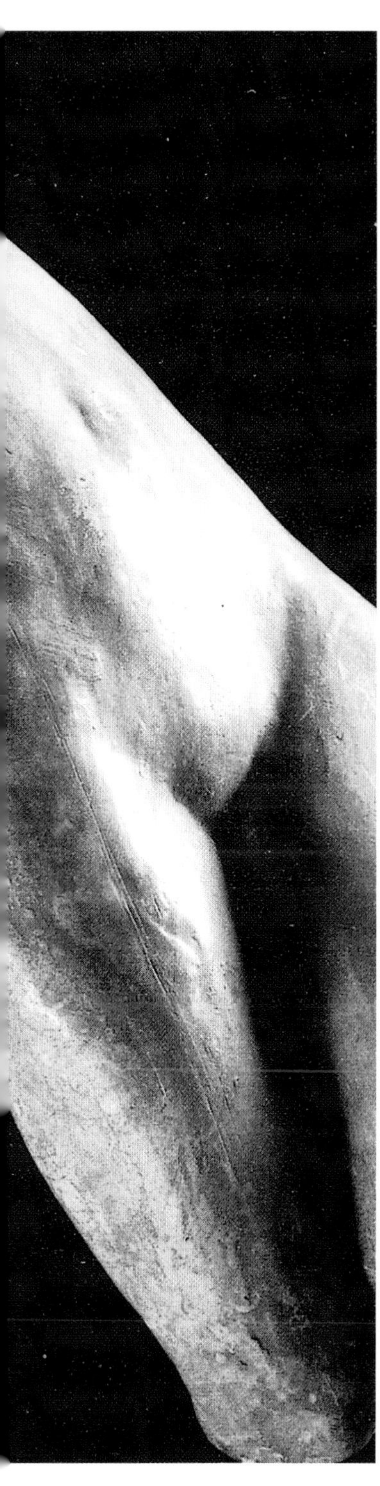

France's defeat in the war with Prussia had brought with it the fall of the régime. The emperor Napoleon III was deposed, the Second Empire collapsed and the Third Republic inaugurated in its place.
A corresponding change in taste away from the impersonal, rhetorical styles favoured under the Empire provided a cultural climate in which the private, emotional and intimate character of Rodin's art was at least more likely to find a sympathetic audience.

Just as his independent statues began to be exhibited, not without controversy, in Paris he won an important public commission (1880) to sculpt a pair of figuratively decorated doors for a new art museum - subsequently to become known as the *Gates of Hell* (3). The state provided Rodin with a large, well-equipped studio in Paris, as well as coal

24 Torso of Adèle

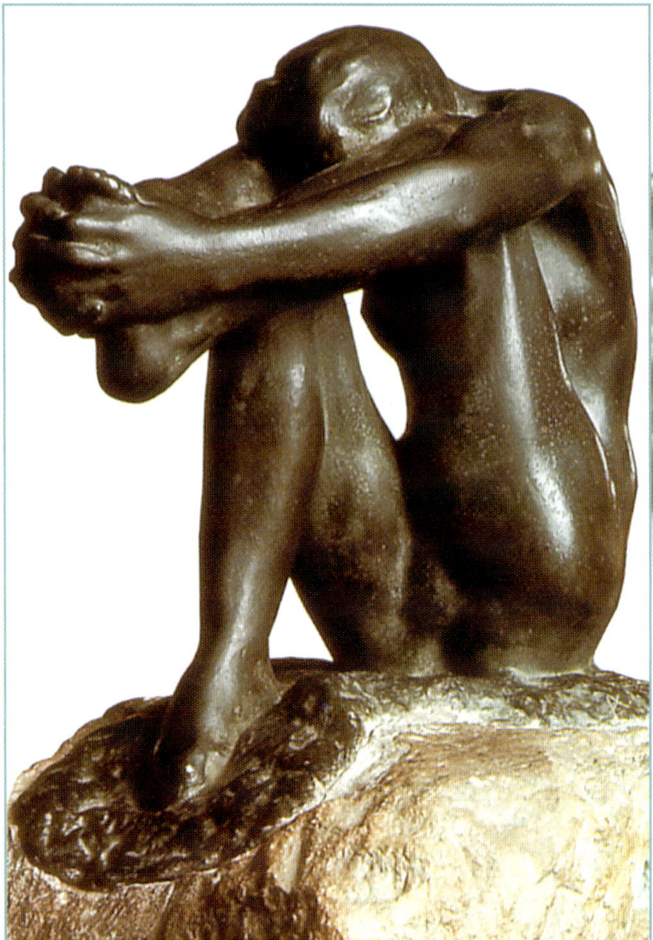

25 Crouching woman 1880-82, bronze

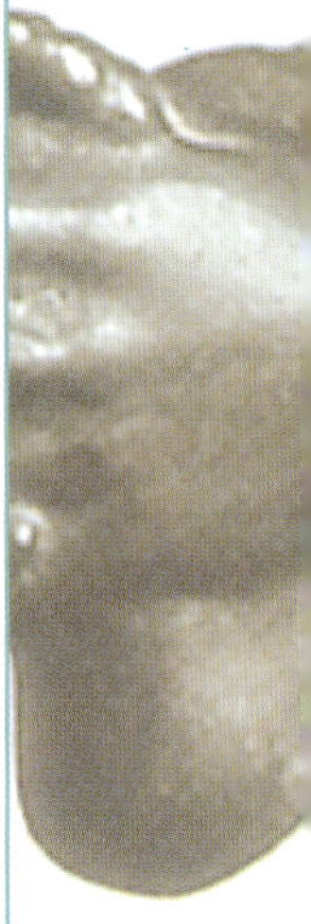

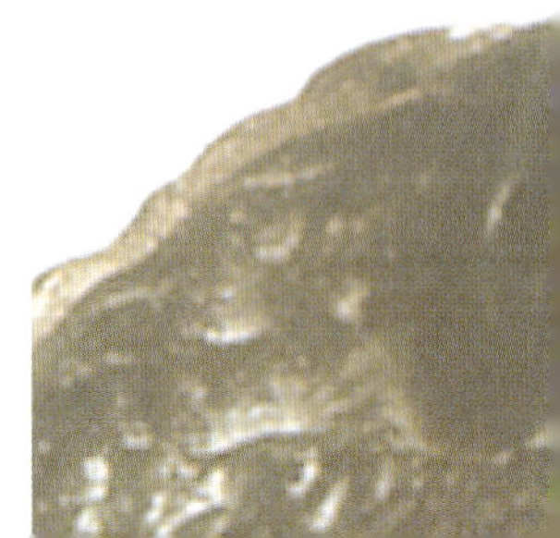

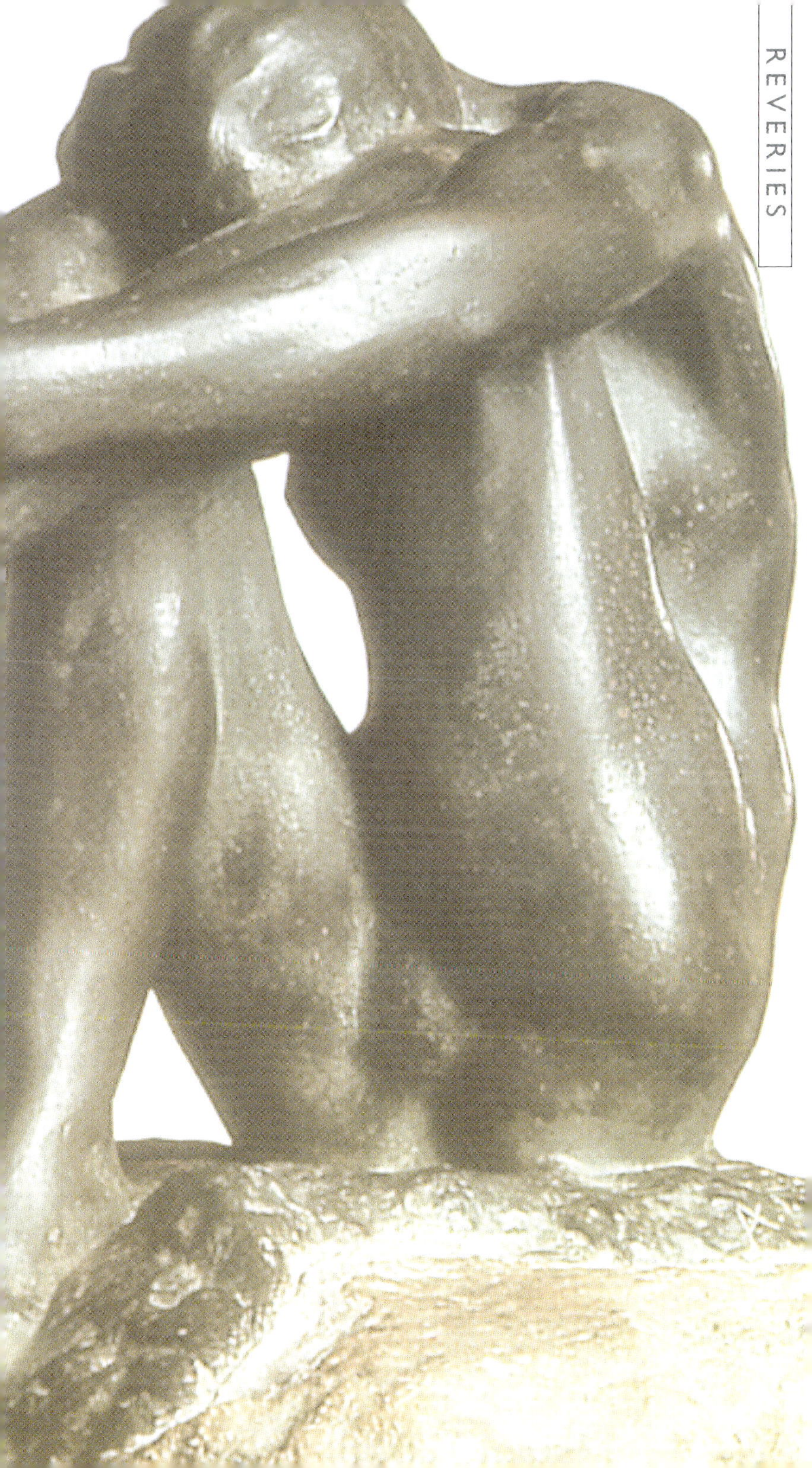

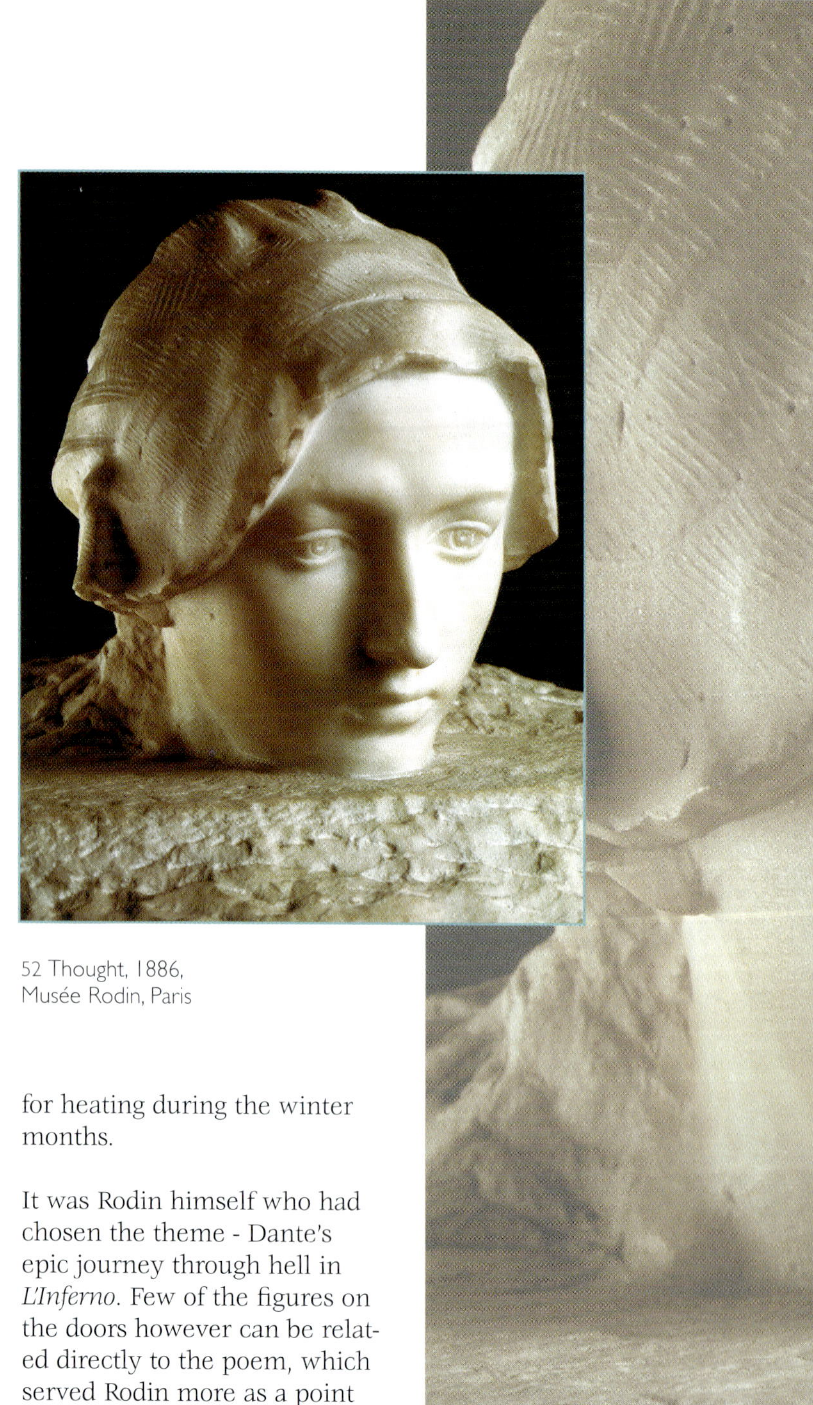

52 Thought, 1886,
Musée Rodin, Paris

for heating during the winter months.

It was Rodin himself who had chosen the theme - Dante's epic journey through hell in *L'Inferno*. Few of the figures on the doors however can be related directly to the poem, which served Rodin more as a point

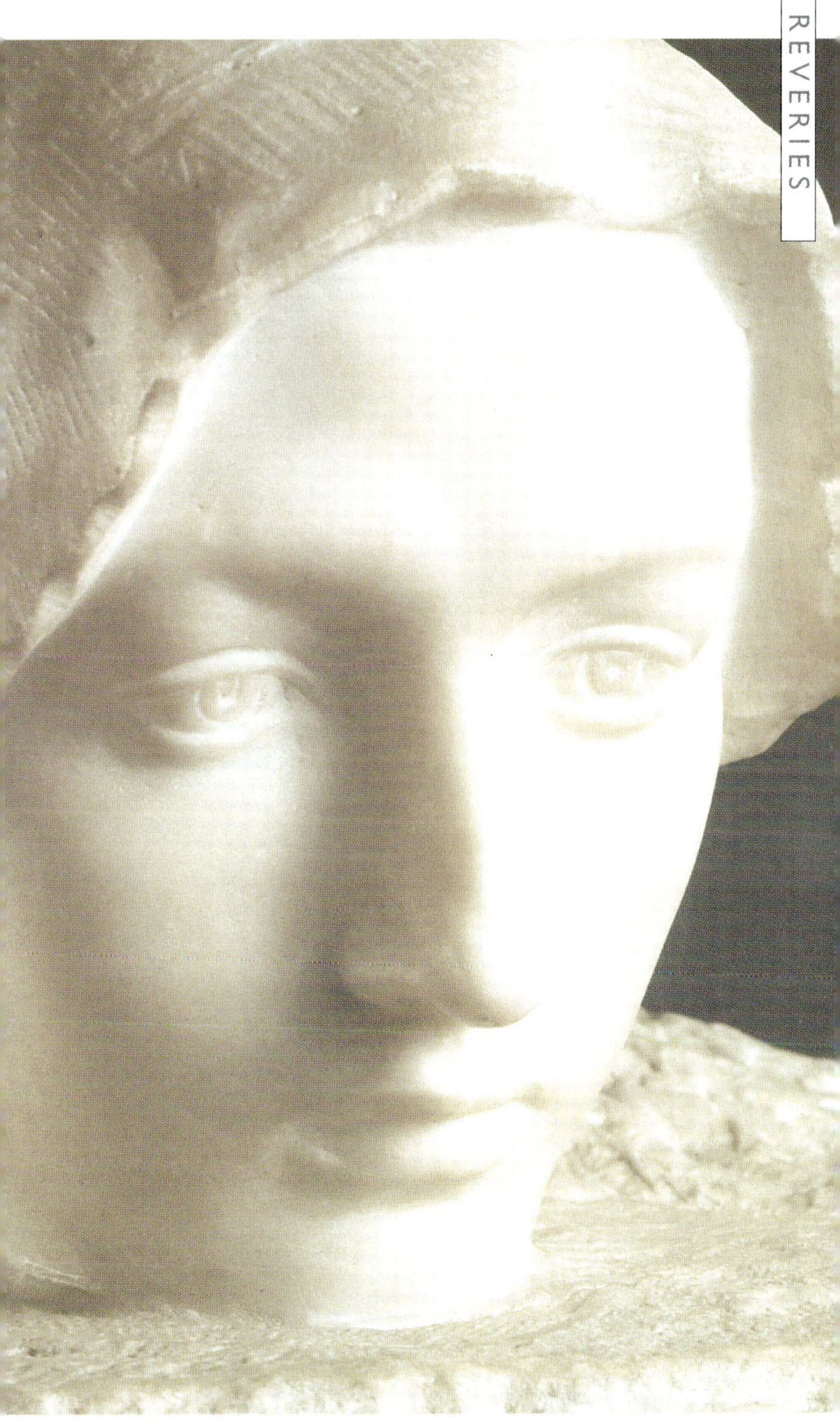

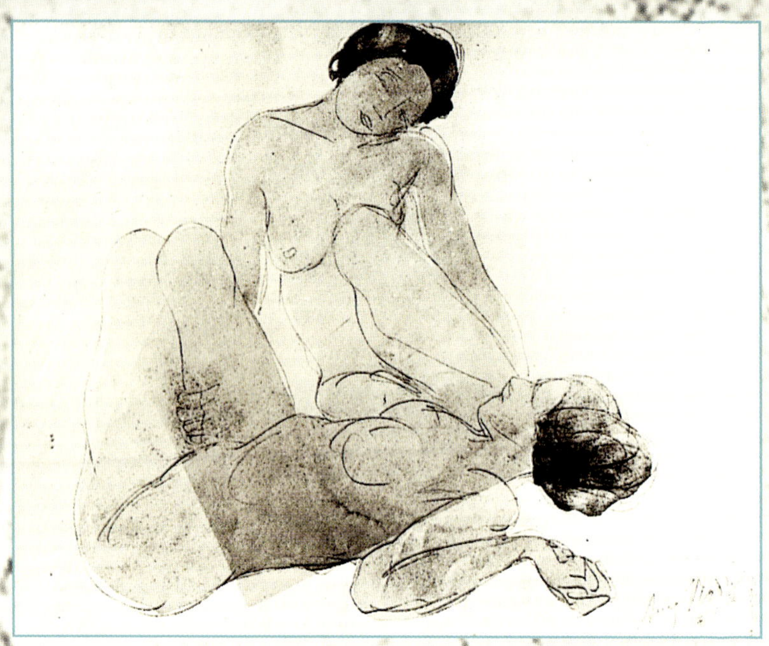

27 Drawing

of departure than a programme to be followed. The gates, in other words, became the expression of Rodin's private vision of tormented humanity. The initial inspiration for the project was acutely pessimistic: the human form was to become the expressive vehicle for inconsolable spiritual distress. The doors are presided over by three figures at the top, who are about to enter the underworld, and by the figure of the *Thinker*, representing the poet himself - powerless and alone as he contemplates the vortex of suffering and anguish beneath. Rational orderings of space, scale and narrative have been dissolved as figures and setting define themselves in terms of fluid, energised despair. Most chillingly, there are no devils on the doors - the source of all this pain is self-inflicted; and there is no redemption.

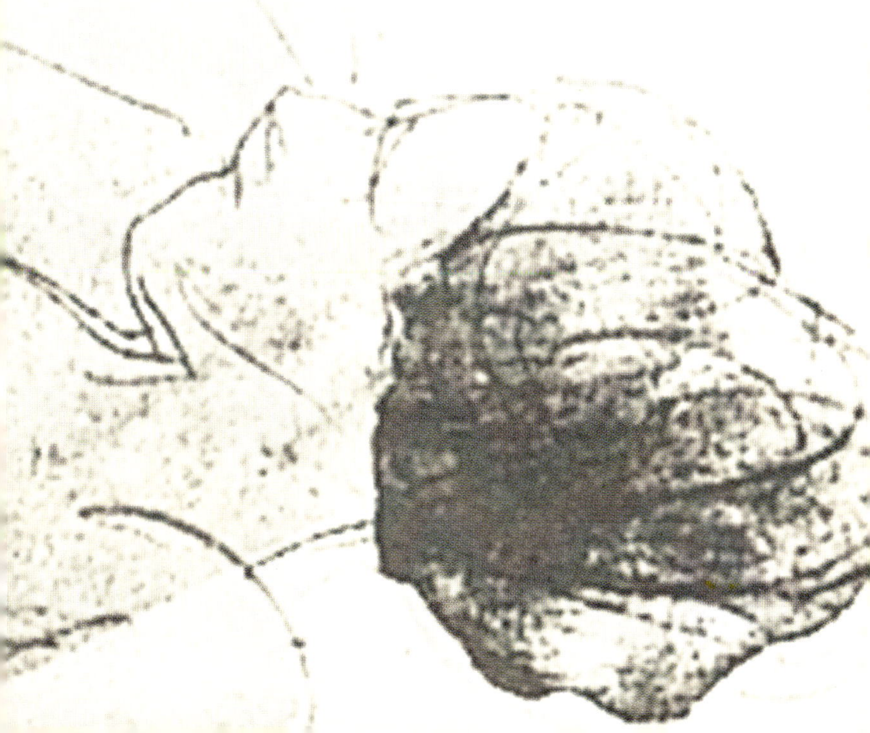

Over many years Rodin experimented with them, constantly adding or adapting the figures (186 in all). Many were later enlarged and recast as independent pieces. The project was to remain unfinished at Rodin's death (1917); but it was while working on the Gates, in 1883, that he met Camille Claudel, twenty years his junior. She was one of a group of students who had come to his studio to learn from him. It was at this point that Rodin's work began to celebrate overtly sexual subjects and to parade erotic sources of inspiration.

In many ways she was an ideal companion for him; not simply because she too had magnificent blue eyes nor that her family also disapproved of her pursuing an artistic career. Spirited, independent-minded, passionate she was more than gifted in her own right as a sculptress. The writer Octave Mirbeau, a friend of Rodin's, described her as "A rovolt of nature, a woman
56 of genius". Their affair lasted for fifteen years.

28 Drawing

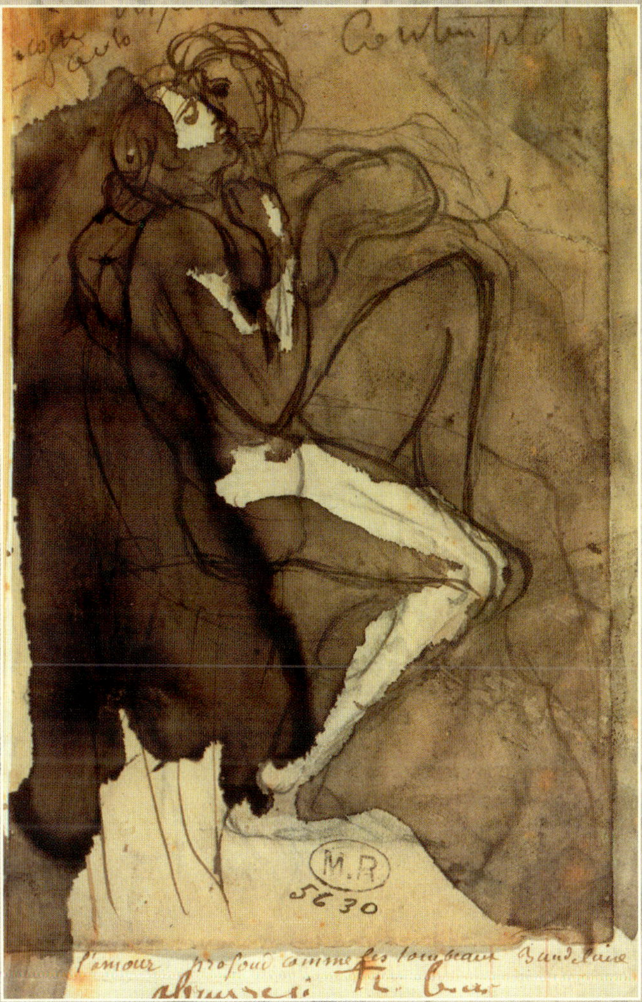
M.R
5630
l'amour profond comme les tombeaux Baudelaire

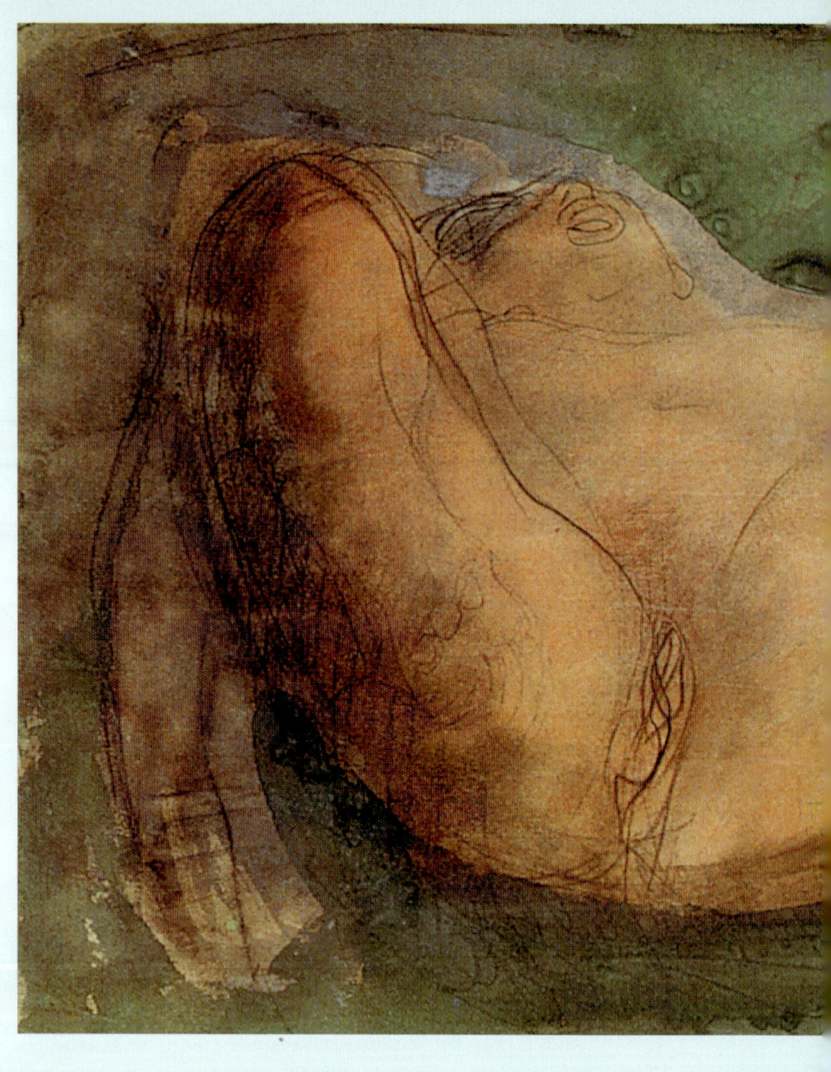

29 Before creation, 1900, watercolour

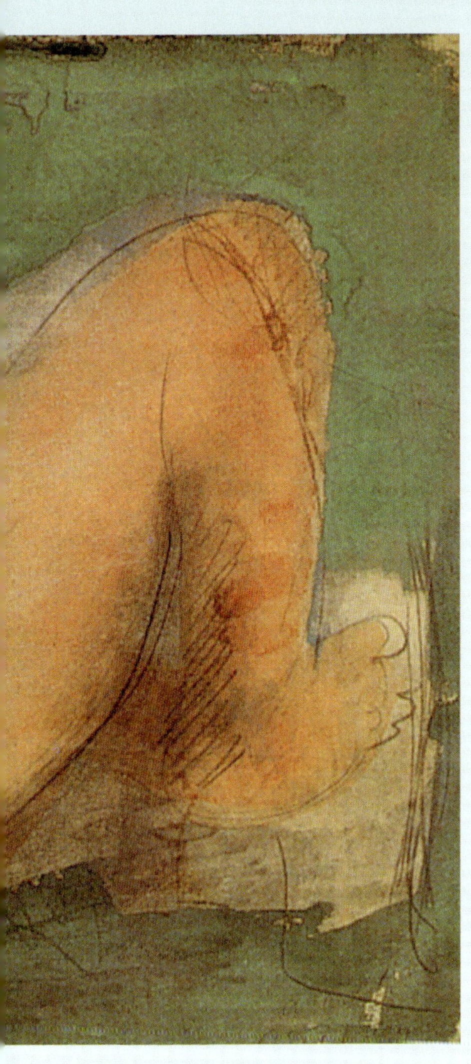

Through most of the 1880s and 1890s Camille Claudel's impact on Rodin's creative life was far out of the ordinary. She seems to have precipitated its transformation. For four years she worked as Rodin's permanent assistant on the Gates, after which she pursued her own independent career. Erotically conceived figures now began to take their places in the scheme for the doors. Many, in addition to Paolo and Francesca in *The Kiss*, were subsequently turned into independent works - *Fugit Amor - 8, Paolo and Francesca - 9, Meditation - 22, Torso of Adèle - 24, Crouching woman - 25* (15, 19). Camille Claudel also modelled for a number of other works: *Thought - 26, Danaid - 20, Head of Camille Claudel - 21* (20, 22). She is like none other of the many women connected with Rodin. Of all his muses she was the most fecund.

30 Entwined couple, ('The War of love'), lead on paper

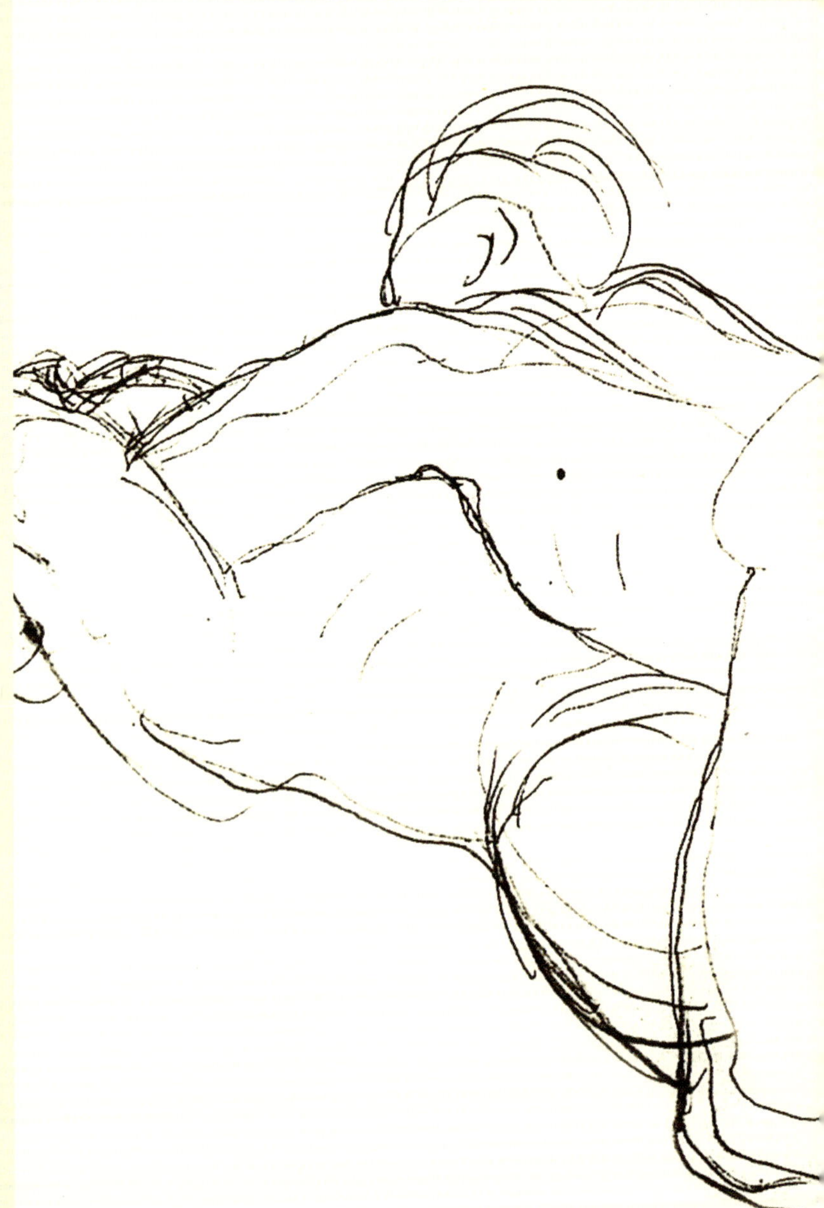

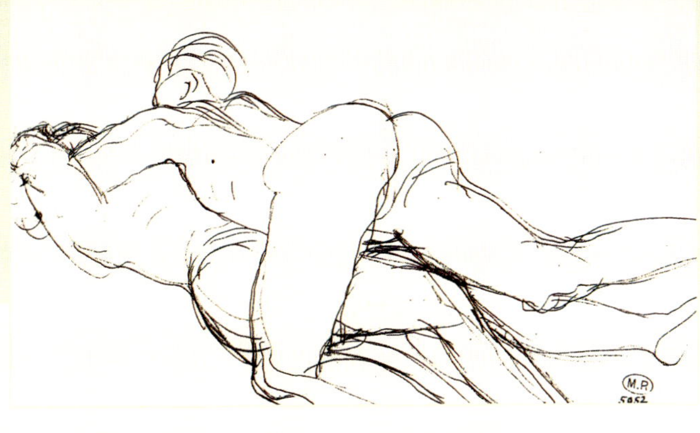

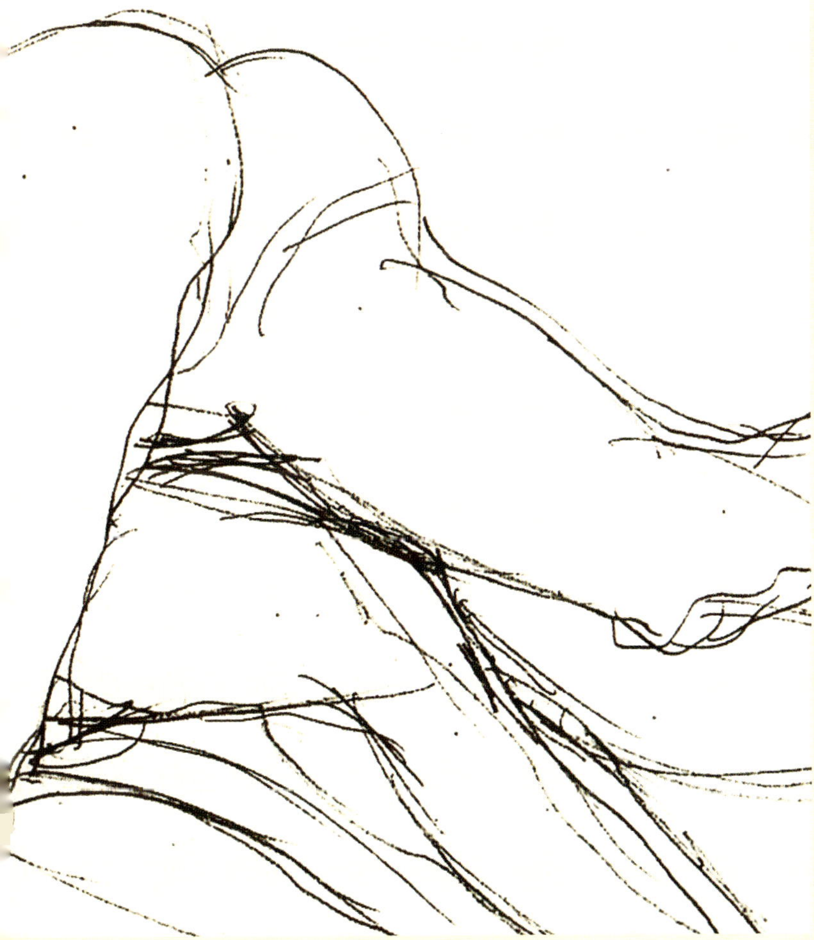

Inevitably Rose suffered; and there were, it is said, many jealous confrontations between the two women. Rodin however, never lived openly with Camille even if for protracted periods he did stay away from Rose. Ultimately it seems that Camille Claudel probably finished the relationship because of Rodin's refusal to leave Rose. Whatever the case, her life after Rodin was one of cruel suffering: she spent the last thirty years of her life in a mental asylum (she died in 1943). Her brother, the poet Paul Claudel never forgave Rodin and described him (understandably) in unflattering but also familiar terms: "... he had the big, bulging eyes of a lecher. When he worked he had his nose right on the model and the clay. Did I say his nose? A boar's snout, rather, behind which lurked a pair of icy blue pupils." (In fairness it should be noted that Rodin was extremely shortsighted and needed to get close to his models).

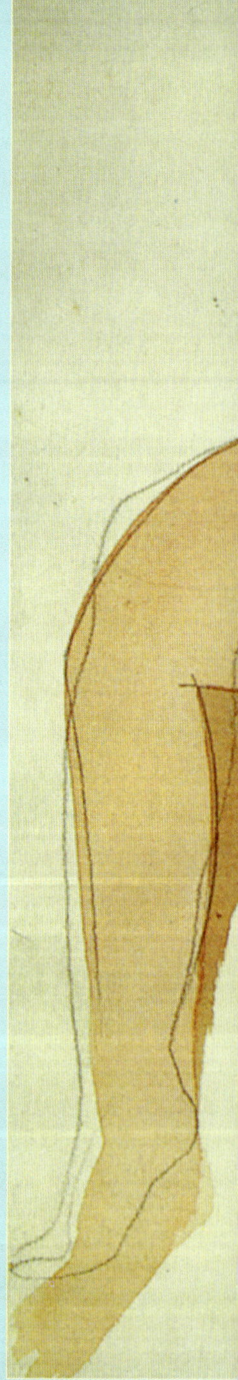

31 Woman on her back, front view, clothes hitched up over her open legs, 1900, lead and watercolour

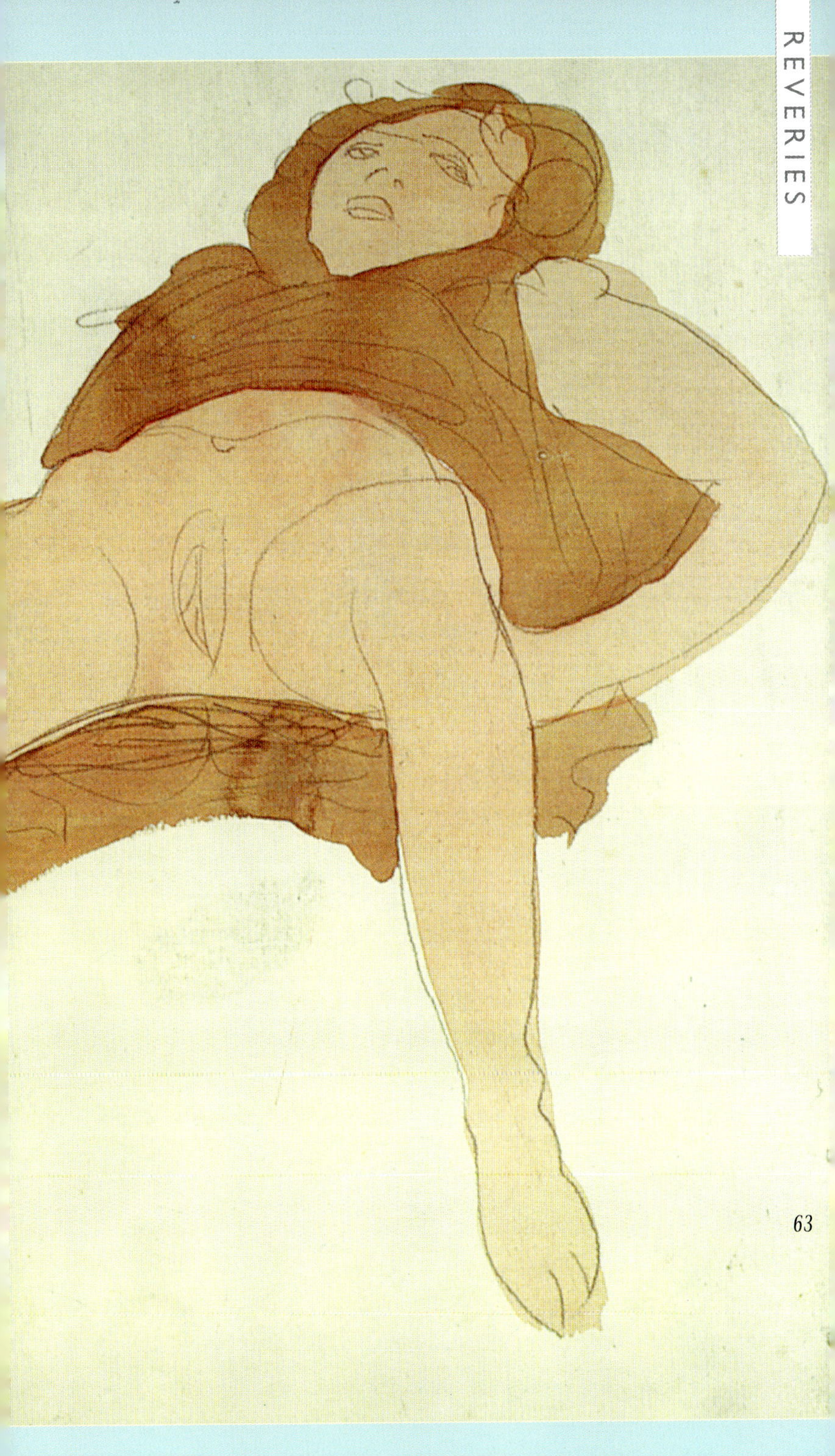

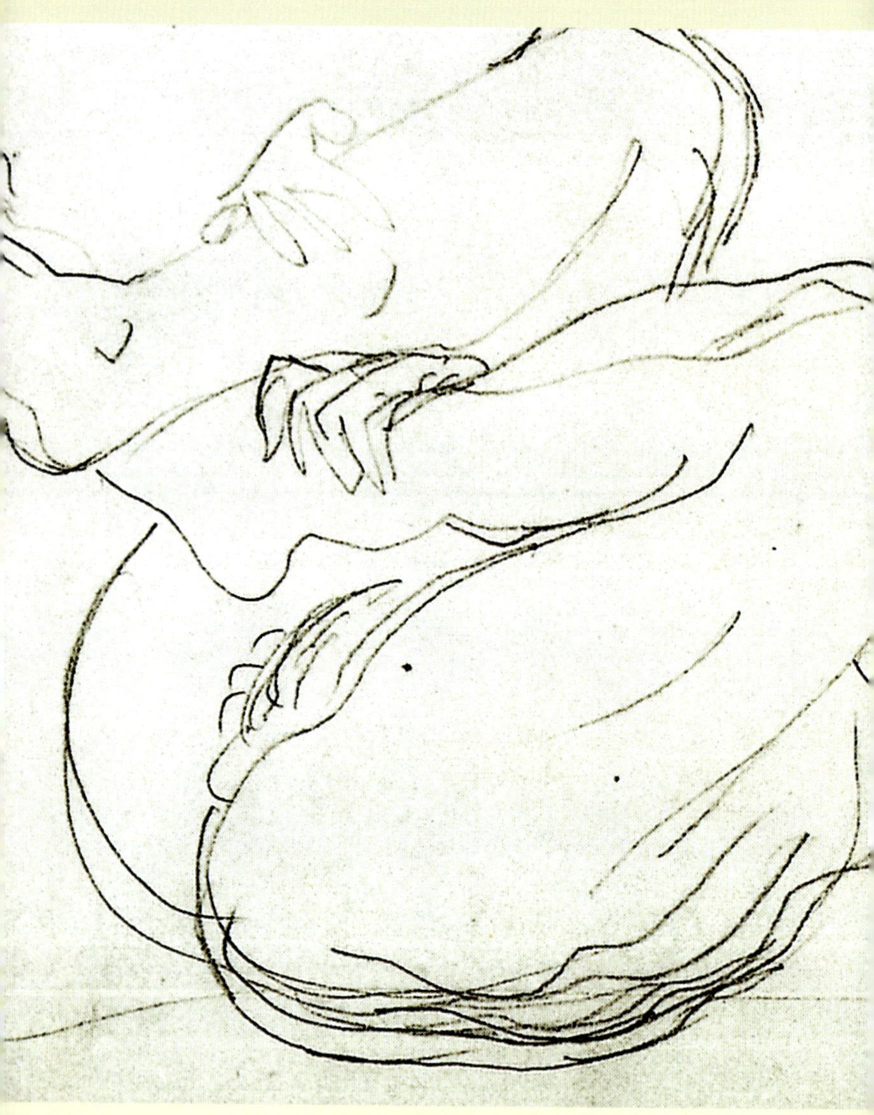

32 Nude woman - on her back, legs raised and folded, lead on paper

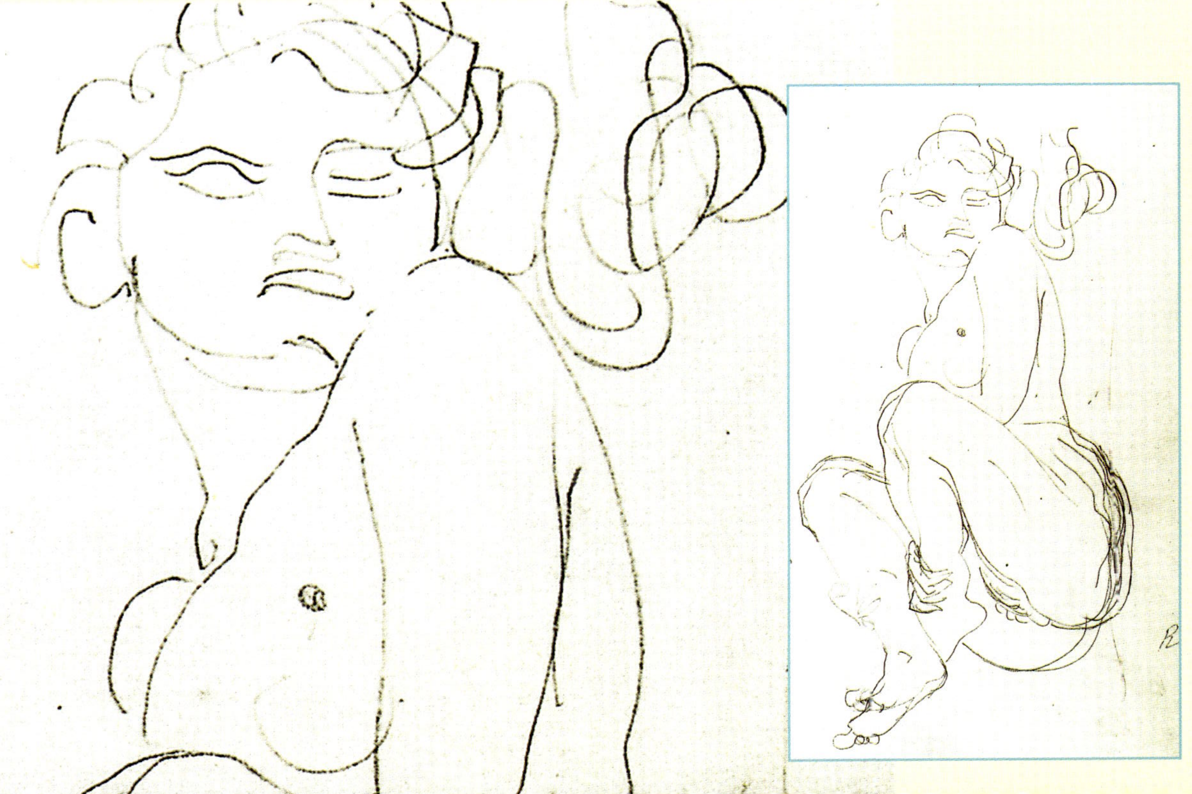

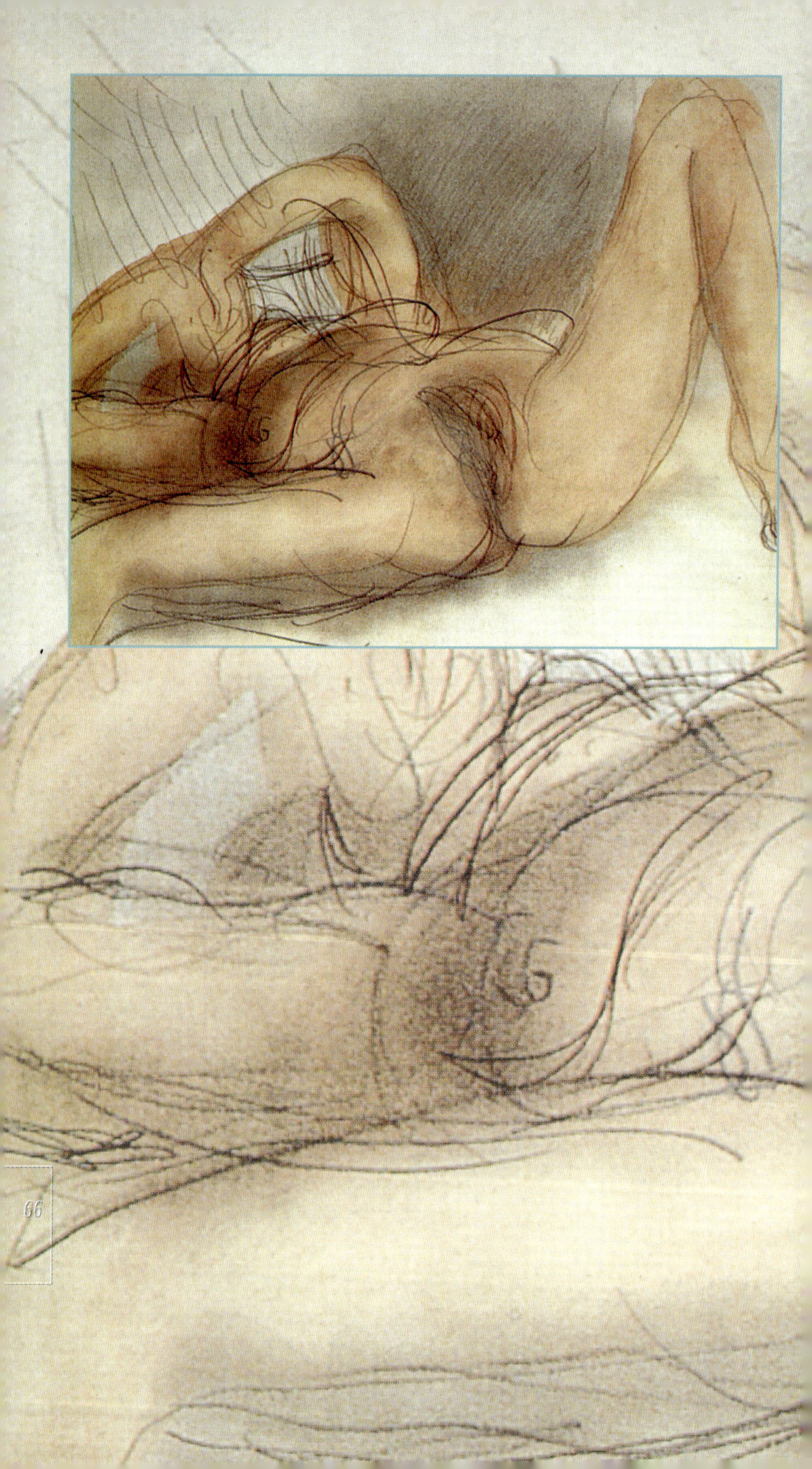

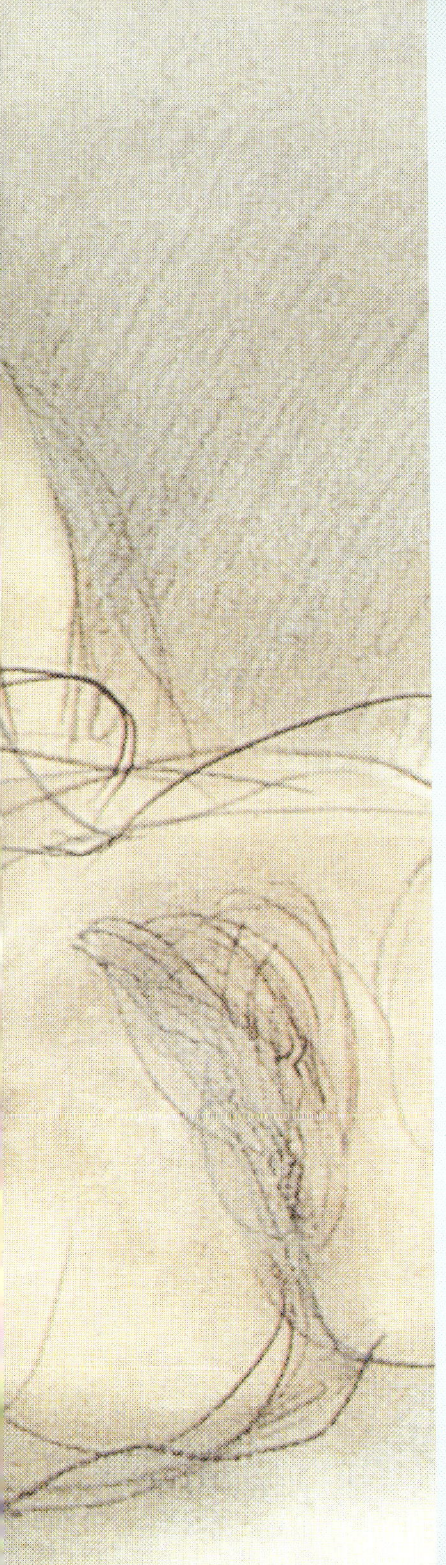

Both women then were broken against his ego - the one punished for her loyalty: never abandoned totally but often ignored, the other unhinged because his love was not exclusive. Other women (notably the British painter Gwen John), and Rodin's son by Rose, also suffered.

FAME AND FORTUNE

The end of their relationship in 1898, as mentioned above, coincided with a period of professional tribulation for Rodin. He responded by showing *The Kiss* and the *Balzac* as we have seen. Two years later, in an even more bullish gesture, Rodin displayed 150 of his works at a privately built pavilion close to the Exposition Universelle that was held in Paris in 1900.

Rodin raised 150,000 francs to build the pavilion which was erected next to the vast area set aside for the official exhibition. The structure was later moved to his garden in

33 Nude woman on her Back with open legs

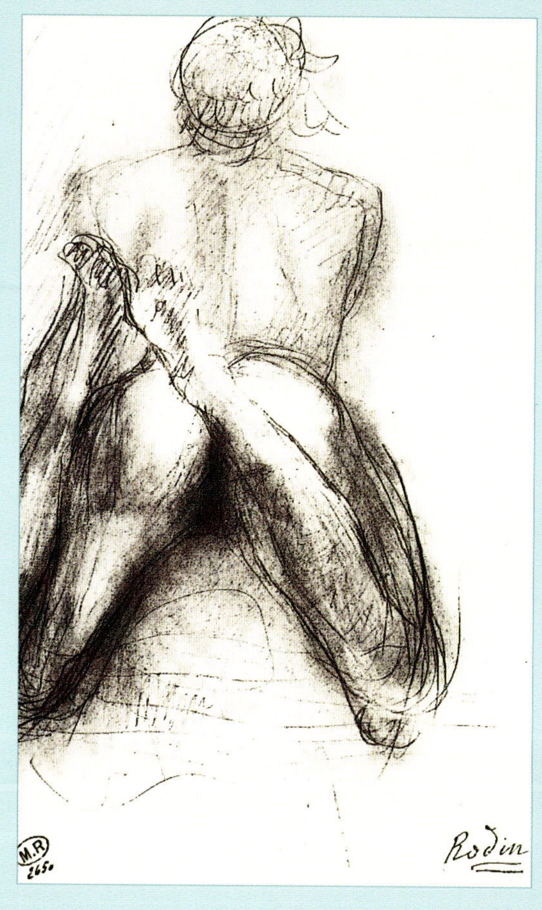

34 Nude woman lying on her stomach, feet raised, lead and charcoal on paper

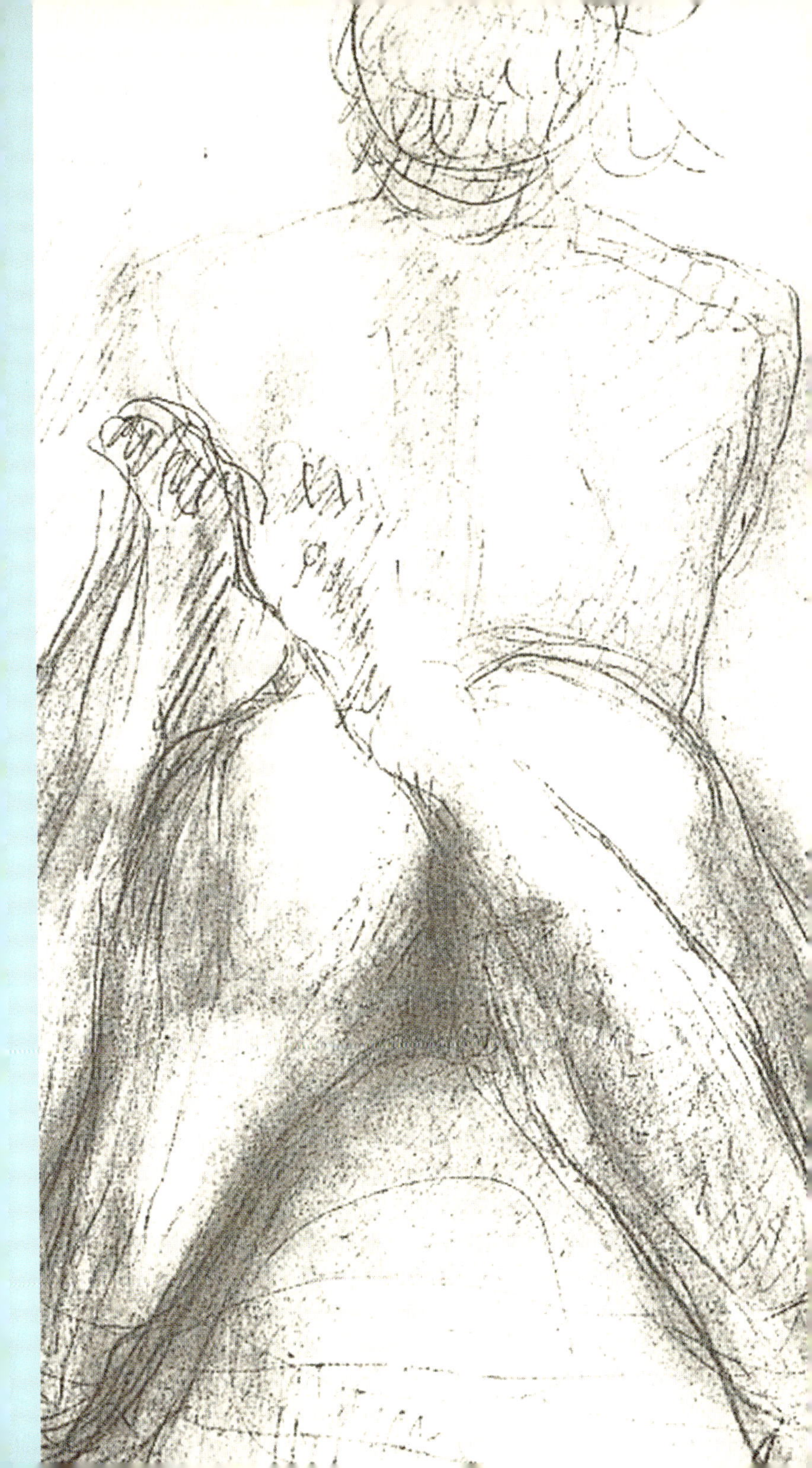

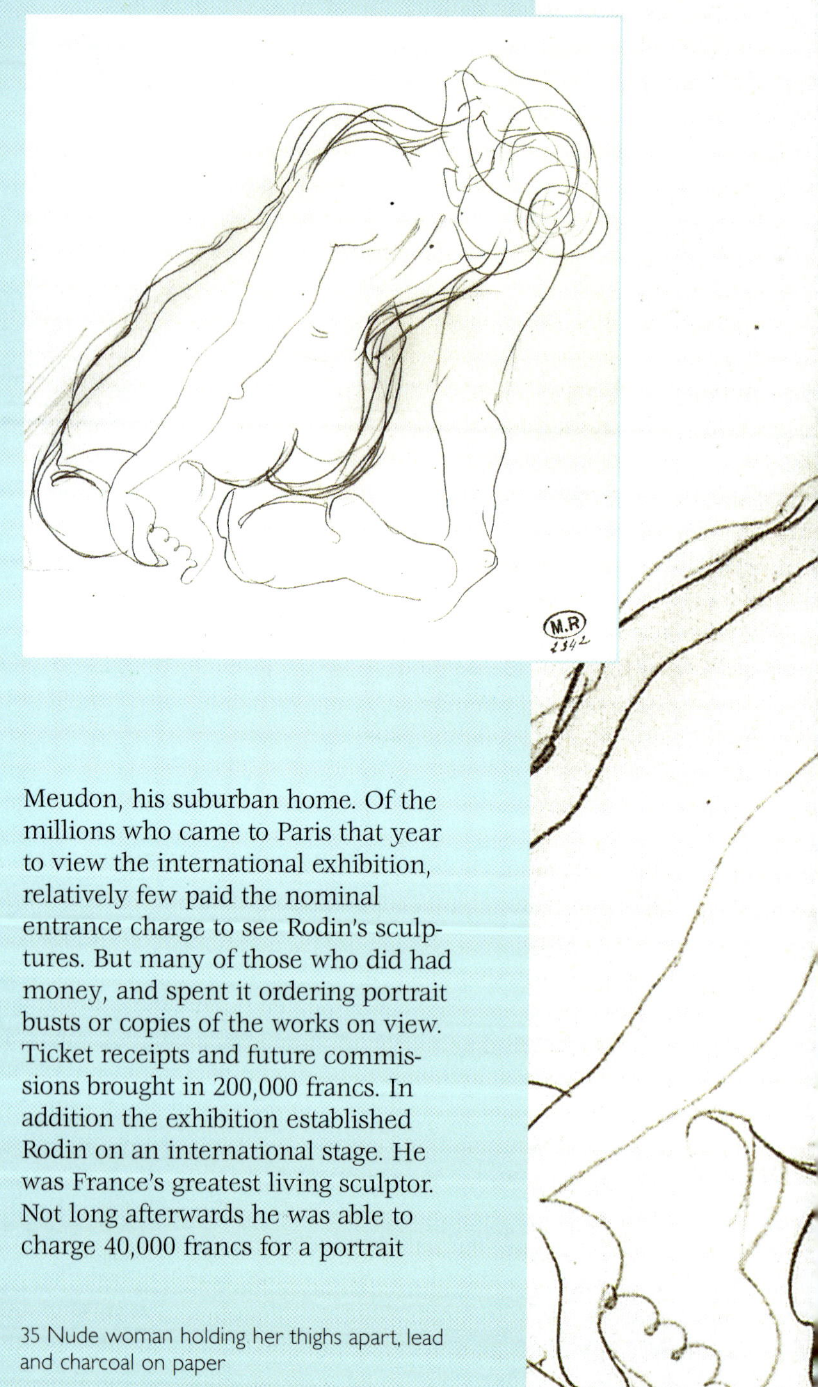

Meudon, his suburban home. Of the millions who came to Paris that year to view the international exhibition, relatively few paid the nominal entrance charge to see Rodin's sculptures. But many of those who did had money, and spent it ordering portrait busts or copies of the works on view. Ticket receipts and future commissions brought in 200,000 francs. In addition the exhibition established Rodin on an international stage. He was France's greatest living sculptor. Not long afterwards he was able to charge 40,000 francs for a portrait

35 Nude woman holding her thighs apart, lead and charcoal on paper

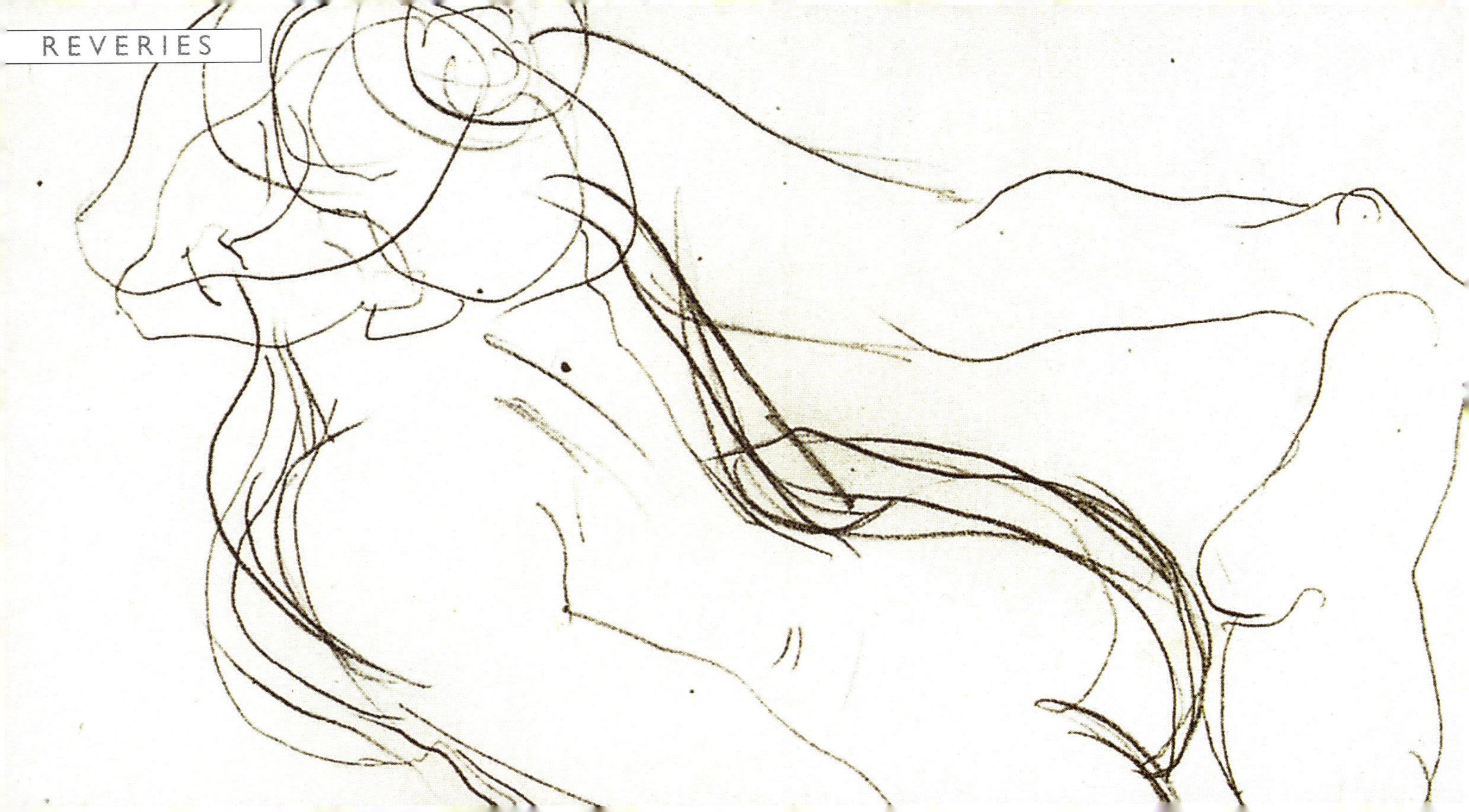

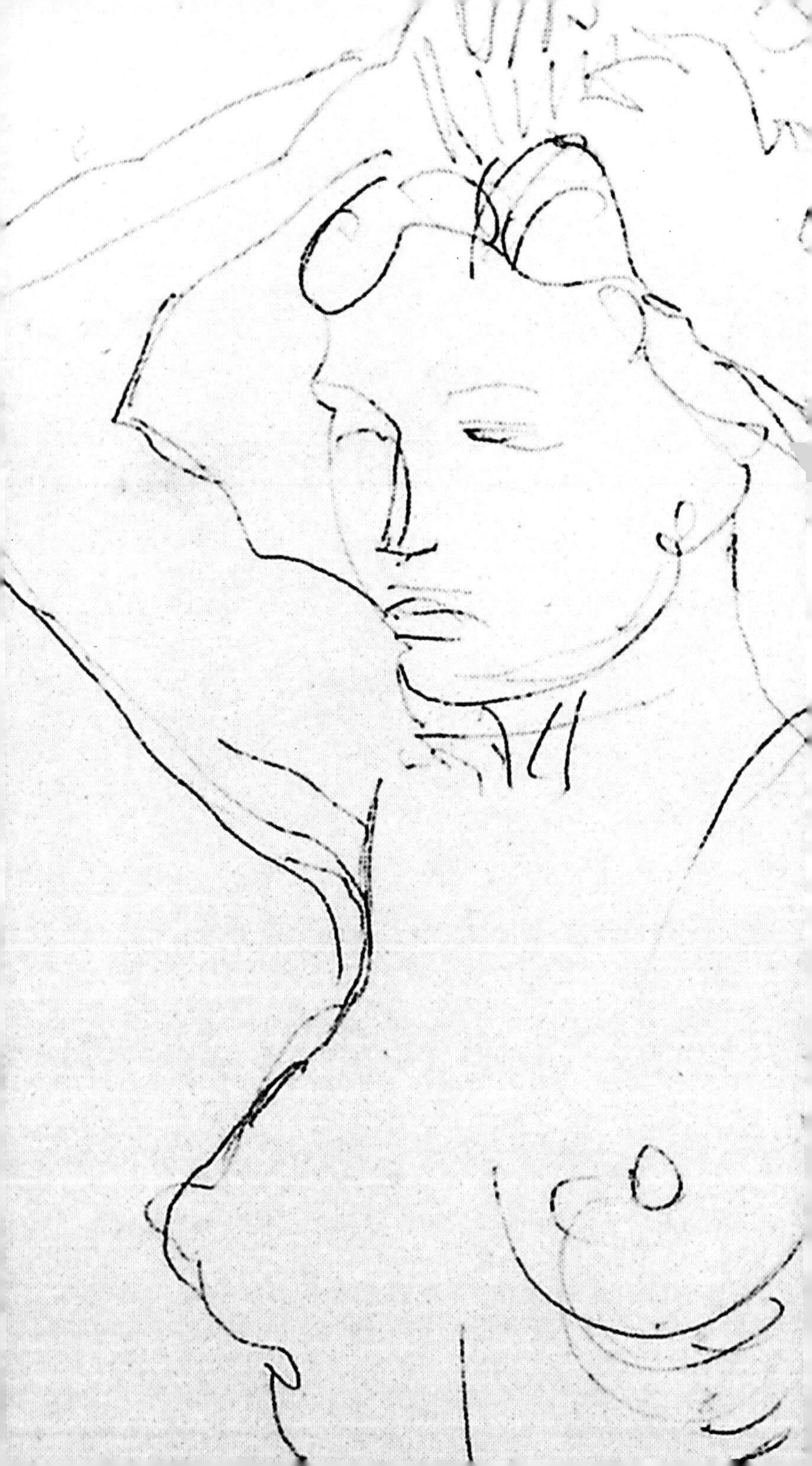

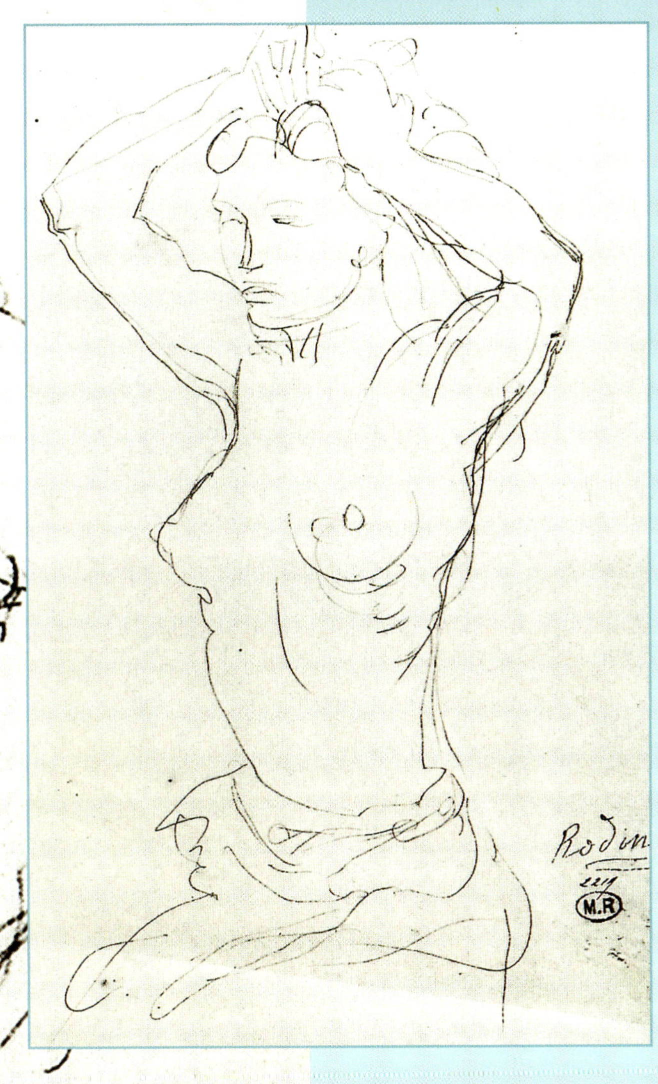

36 Bust of a nude woman, seated, hands in her hair, lead on paper

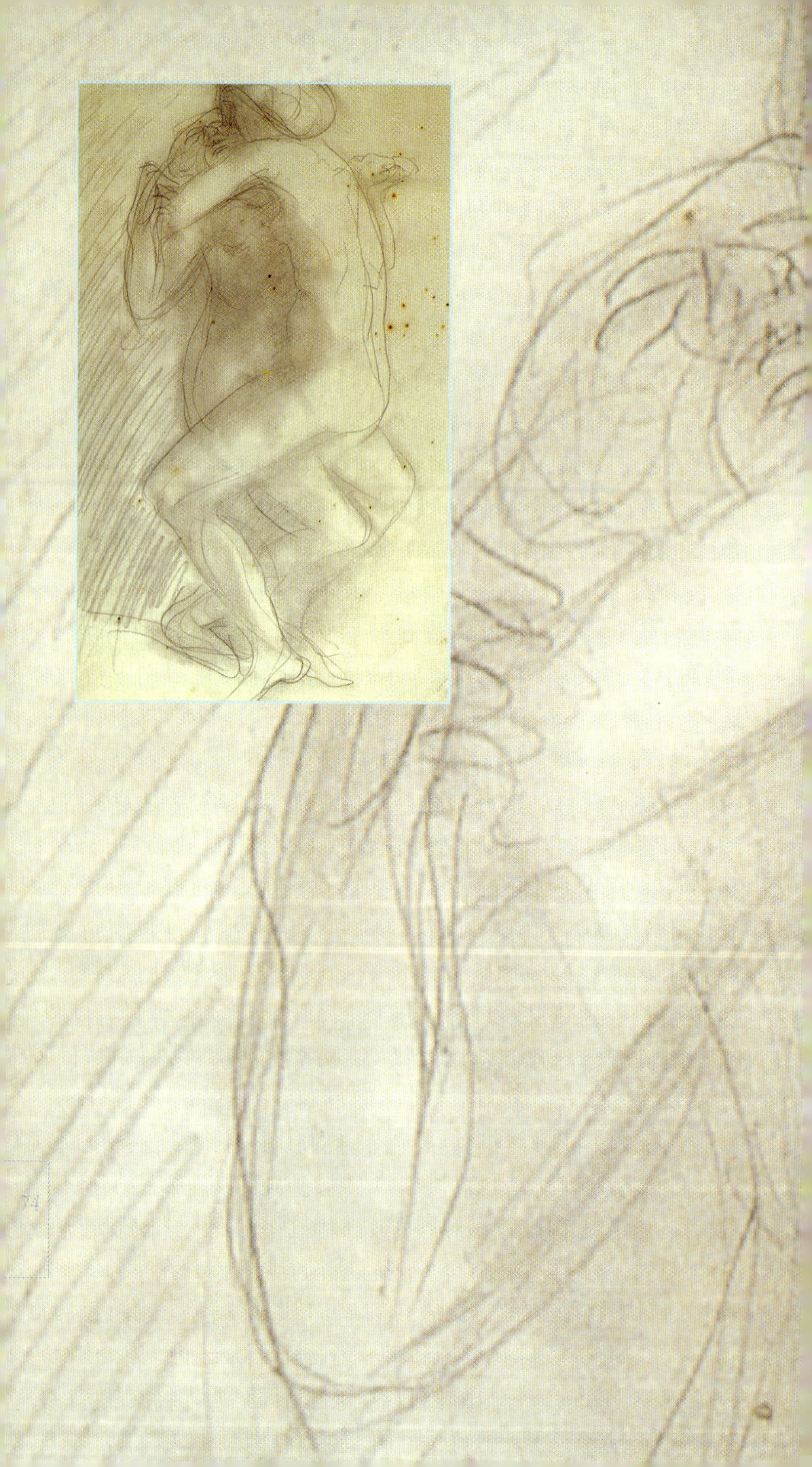

bust (17); royalty paid visits to his studios; Oxford University in England awarded him an honorary doctorate; Cézanne, on meeting him at Monet's house, went down on one knee; art students in England unhitched the horses on his carriage and pulled both him and it along the crowded, central London streets.

With fame and fortune came a relative decline in the number of new, large-scale, original works of sculpture. Rodin employed an even larger studio and supervised the reproduction of many earlier pieces. But arguably the great creative enterprise of his later years was pursued in a different medium altogether - drawing.

RODIN'S LATE DRAWINGS

Rodin had drawn all his life but the drawings he made from around the turn of the century (when he was sixty) to his death in 1917 are utterly distinctive. There are around 8,000 of them. Made either with pencil alone, or with the addition of pen and ink or colour washes, these late drawings are images of the most refined simplicity and concise beauty. They divide into two types: female dancers, in particu-

37 Drawing

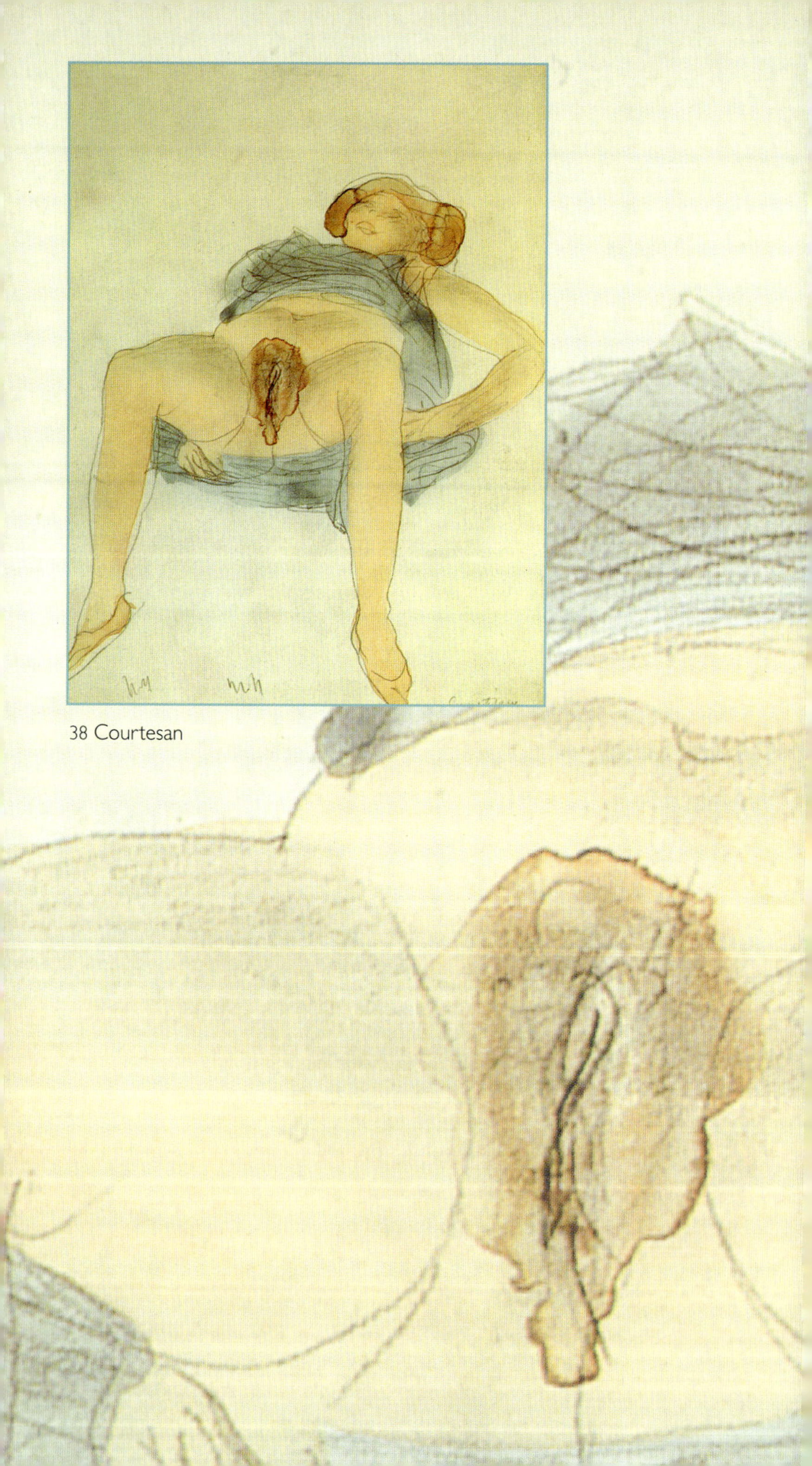

38 Courtesan

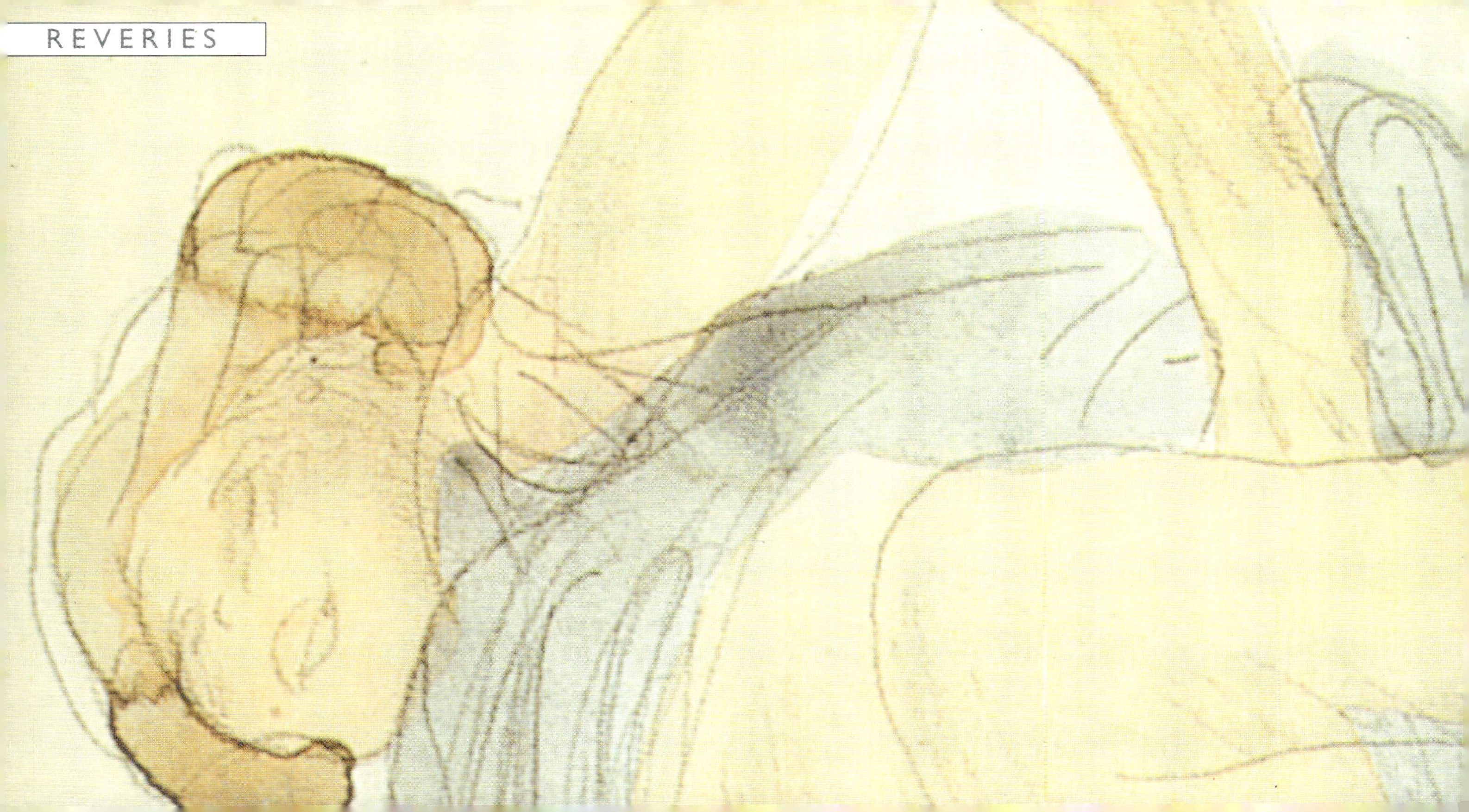

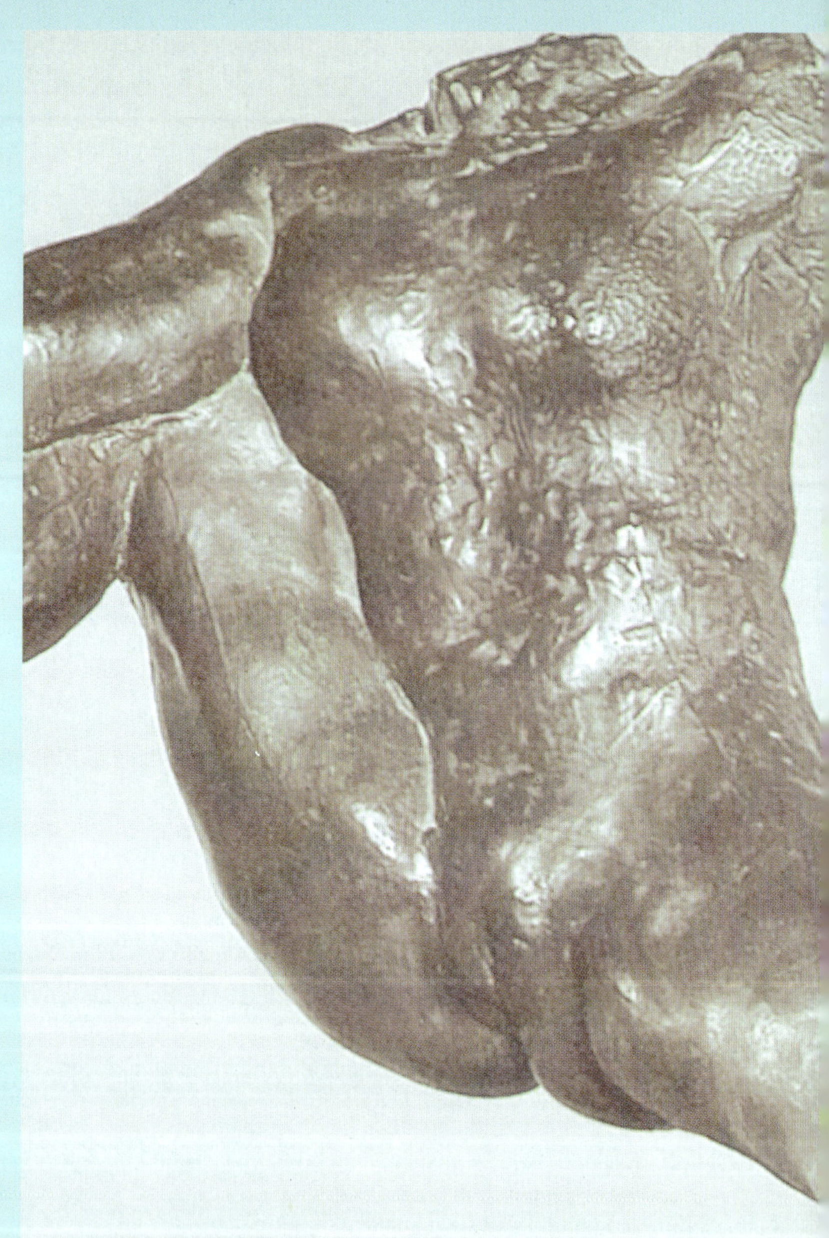

42 Iris

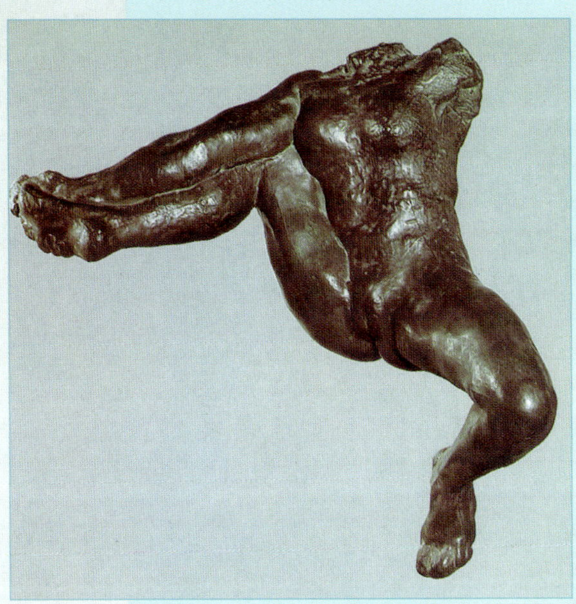

39 Iris, Messenger of the Gods, bronze

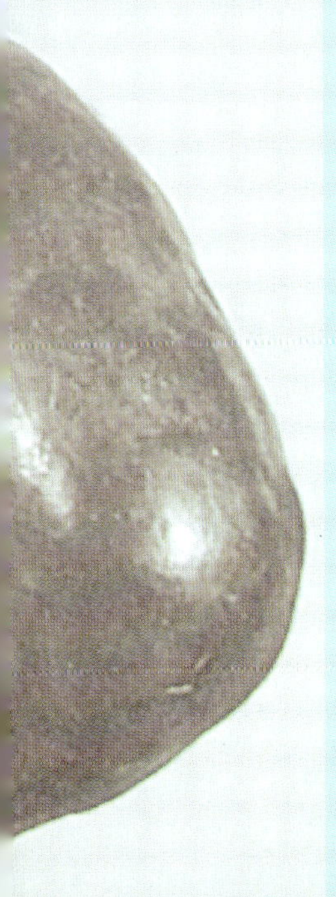

lar Javanese and Cambodian dancers, and nude female models (23, 40). Both types were made very quickly, in pencil, from life; some were worked up later. A few were made by tracing from the original onto another sheet - so as to eliminate superfluous lines as a further means of simplification; some were cut-out and recombined with other figures. This method of working was highly unusual - both for its speed and freedom. Rodin did not look at the page while he was working. Neither did he ask his models to hold any particular pose. Instead he drew as they moved freely around him, letting each finished sheet fall to the floor as he began another. The daring

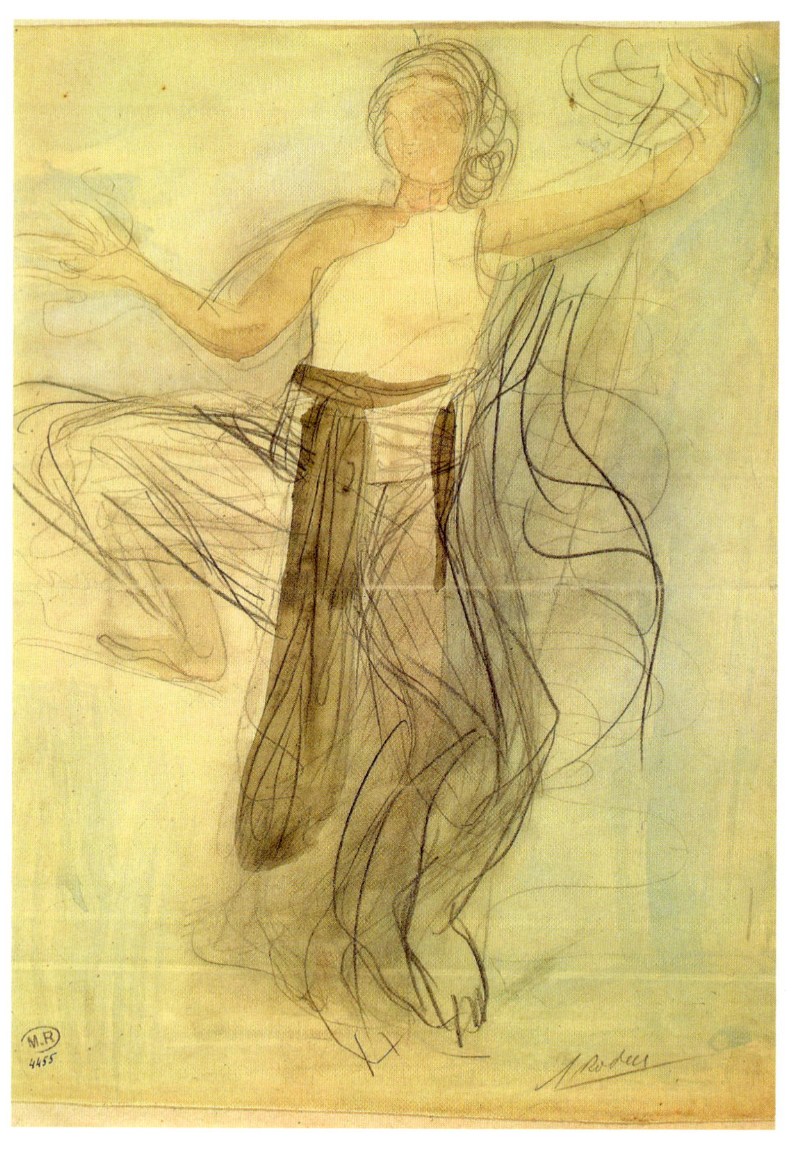

40 Cambodian dancer standing on the left leg with outstretched arms, 1906, graphite stump and watercolour with oiled pencil on buff pencil, Musée Rodin, Paris

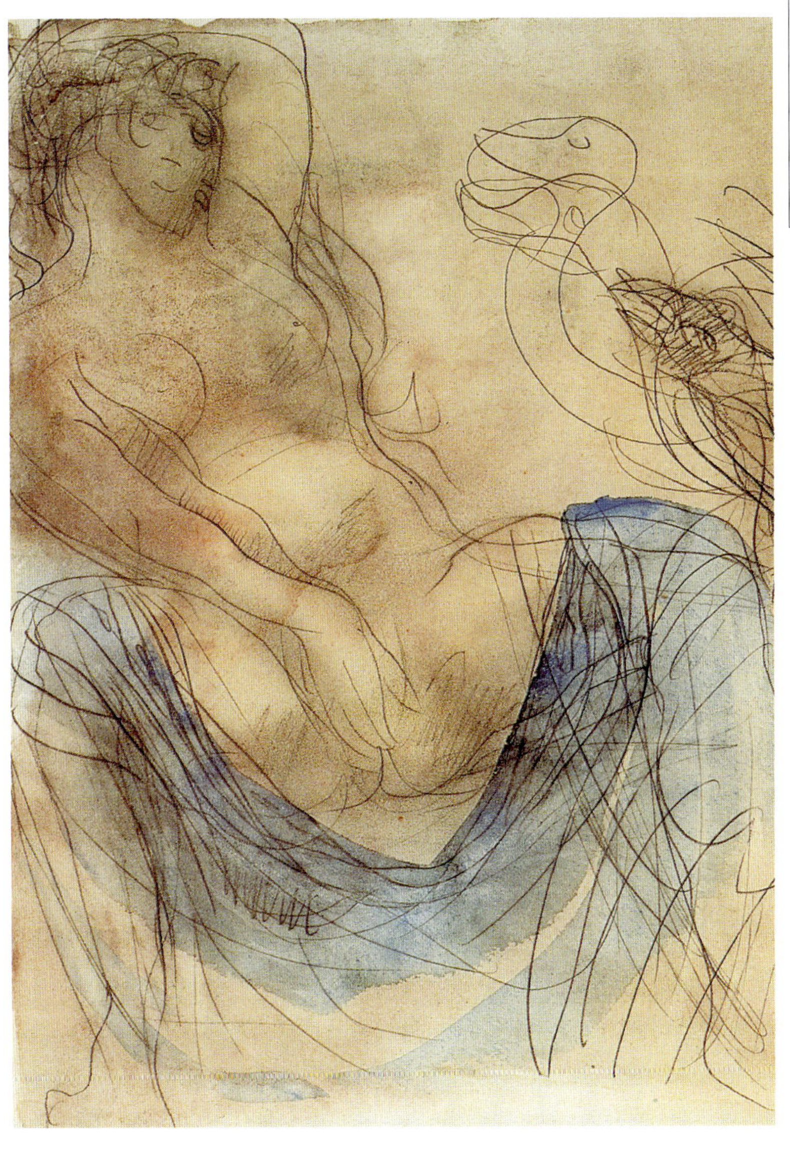

41 Reclining woman, hand between her legs, with a bird, 1910, graphite stump, and watercolour on buff paper, Musée Rodin, Paris

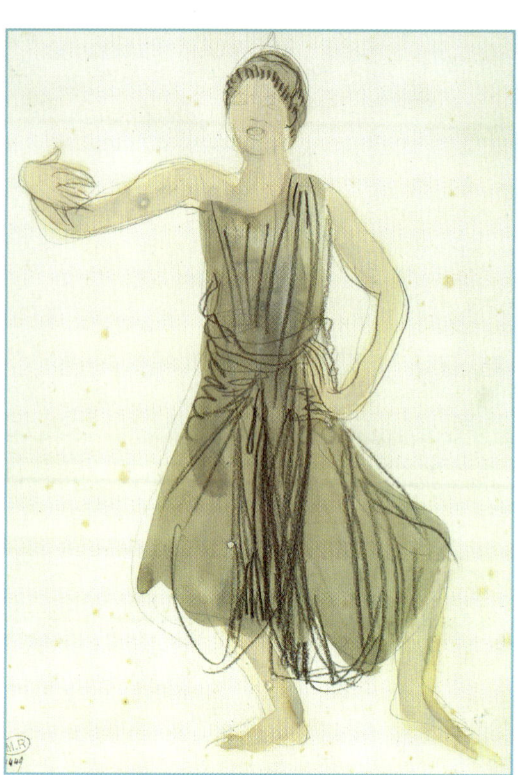

42 Cambodian dancer standing on right leg with her left hand on hip, 1906, graphite, watercolour and gouache with black pencil on buff paper, Musée Rodin, Paris

poses and viewpoints and the bold distortions that resulted are extraordinary.

This very innovative way of working coincided with Rodin's obsession with modern dance during this late period. Writing in an article published in 1912 he claimed that "dance has always had the prerogative of eroticism in our society. In this, as in other expressions of the modern spirit, women are responsible for the renewal." Isadora Duncan, another American dancer called Loie Fuller, Diaghilev, Nijinsky, the Japanese actress Hanako (46) all knew him and posed for him. Isadora Duncan opened a

43 Drawing

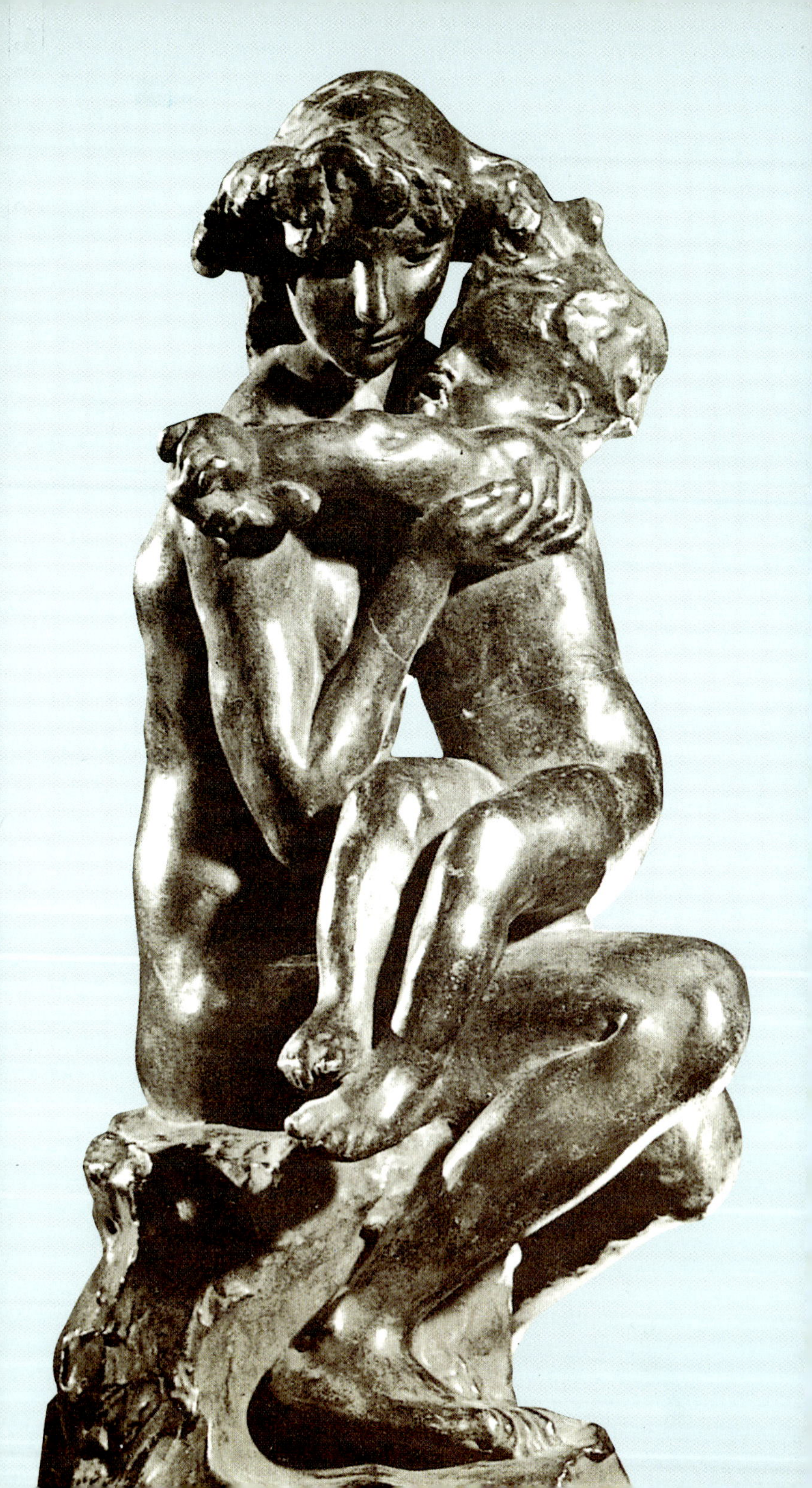

ballet school and brought her students to Rodin's studio so that he could draw them. In 1906 Rodin followed a group of Cambodian dancers from Paris to Marseilles for the same purpose. His ecstatic response to these various dancers' elegant and liberated movement found expression in sculptural form (*Iris* - 39) as well as drawings.

When dancers were not available to draw from Rodin was wealthy enough to employ models. Many of these drawings of nude models are of an intensely erotic nature; the ones illustrated here are among them. They are unlike anything else by his hand.

Rodin had produced erotic drawings at other times and under different circumstances - for book illustrations. He had provided drawings for a privately printed edition of Baudelaire's *Les Fleurs du Mal* (1885) and for a limited folio edition of Octave Mirbeau's *Le Jardin des supplices* (1902); but neither of these even palely matches the later drawings for obsessive, sexual concentration, energy and freedom.

The works by Rodin reproduced in lithograph for Mirbeau's erotic novel do not focus on female pudenda as do the later ones, although they are similar in style. The Baudelaire drawings are also far less explicit and were made in a darker, nervous and more agitated

44 Brother and Sister

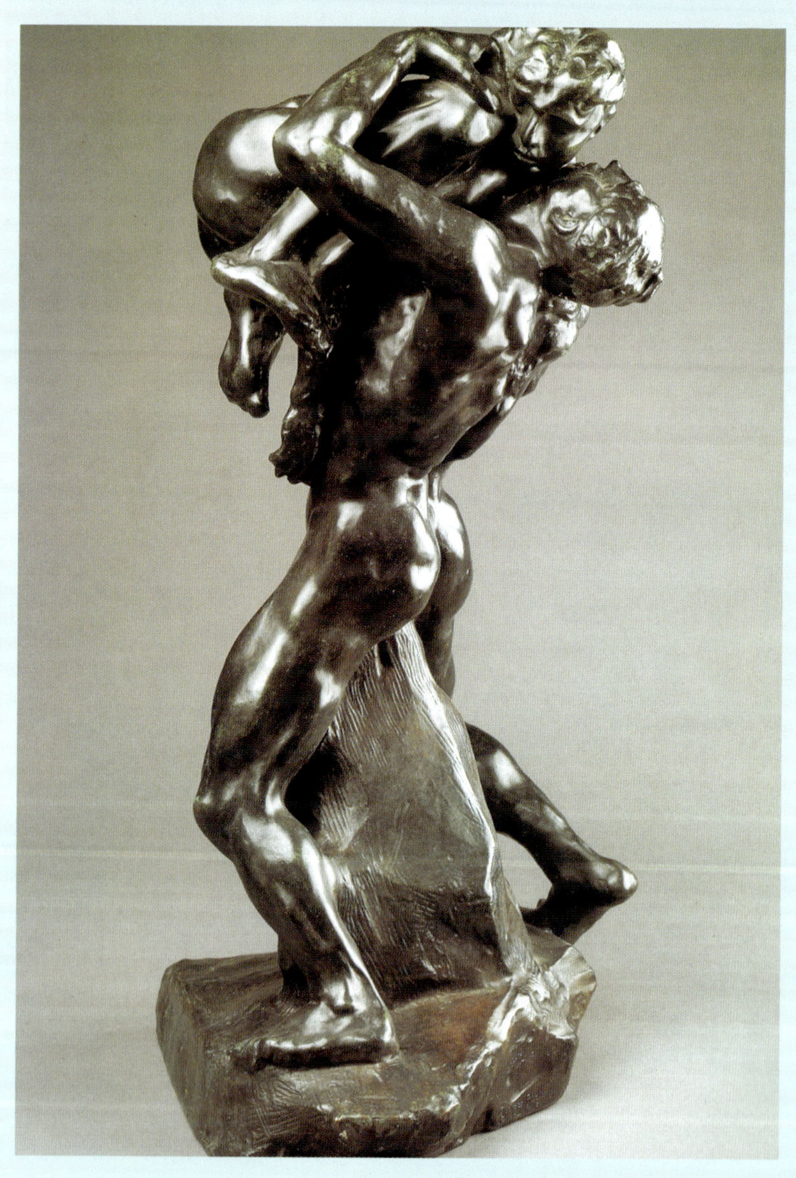

45 Je Suis Belle (I am Beautiful). 1882, marble

graphic style. Certainly the troubled, painful character of these drawings as well as the sculptures made at around the same time are comparable in mood to the tone and atmosphere both of Baudelaire's poetry and the Gates of Hell. It seems reasonable to sense in works such as *Je Suis Belle* (the title is taken from a poem by Baudelaire; both figures may be also found, separately, on the *Gates* - 51) for example, a guilty or morbid erotic vision in which sexual fulfilment remains unattainable. The later drawings display nothing of the self-conscious and virtuosic indulgence in such an oppressive expression of darkness, struggle and godlessness. They are of a different order altogether.

Principally what distinguishes them is their quantity (generally unknown until quite recently); the fact that the vast majority were never exhibited; the innovative methods by which they were made and the uncompromising, obsessive nature of their subject-matter. Nude, female models are drawn, time after time after time, with legs spread apart. The vulva is placed at the centre of the image - this is the fulcrum or focus, as it were, of Rodin's old age. In some, the models masturbate and either mimic or perform acts of lesbian love. Categorically it seems that Rodin had left behind the guilt and torment of the Gates to enter a labial world of uninhibited exuberance and pleasure.

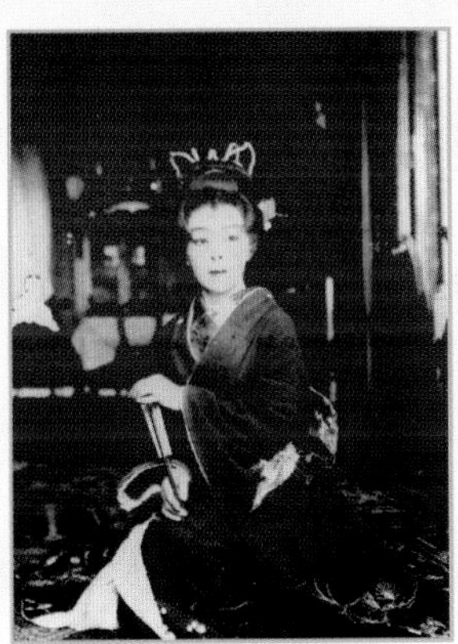

46 Hanako in traditional costume

THE HÔTEL BIRON

The theatre for much of this work and activity was the Hôtel Biron in Paris. Originally an eighteenth-century private residence, it had subsequently been owned by

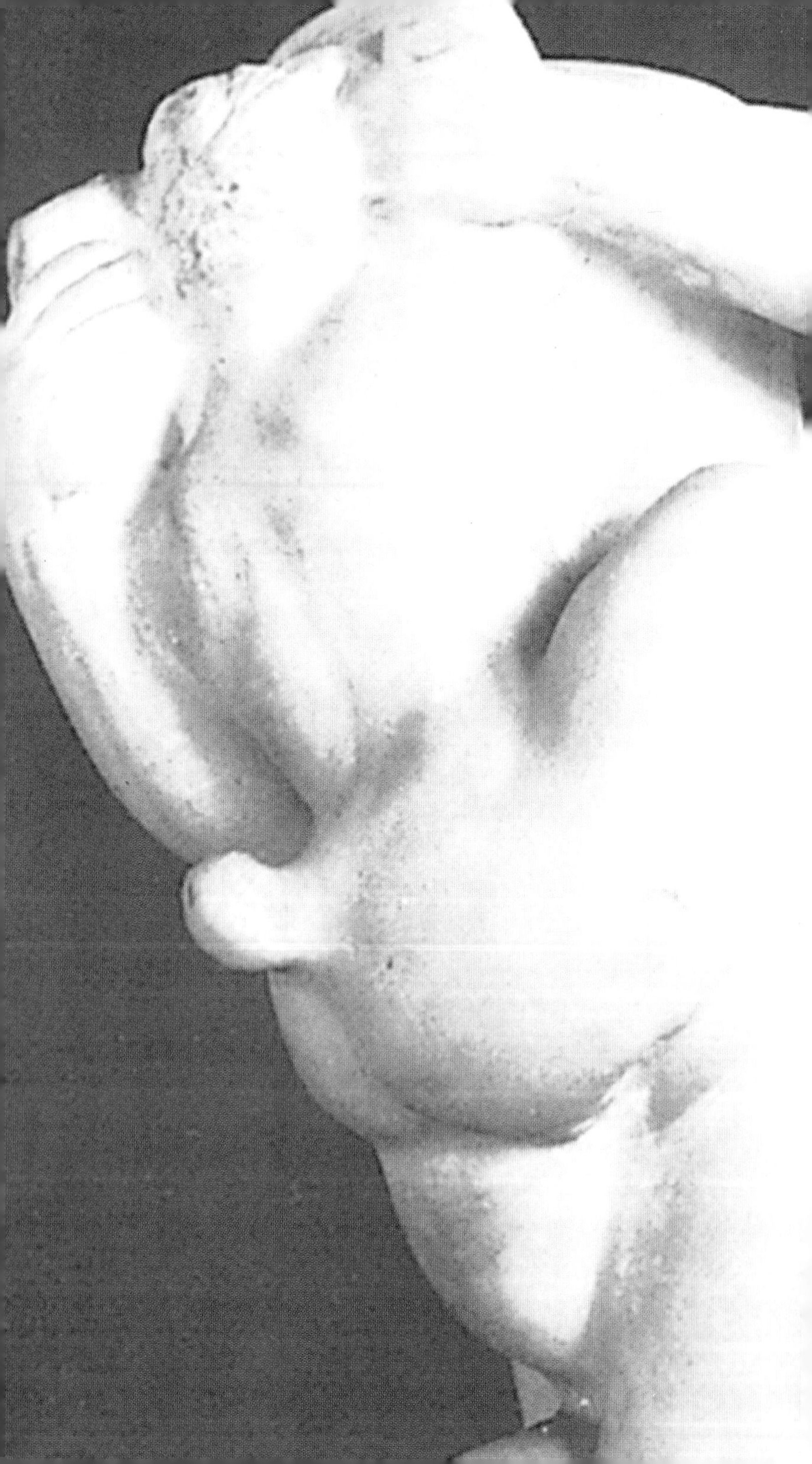

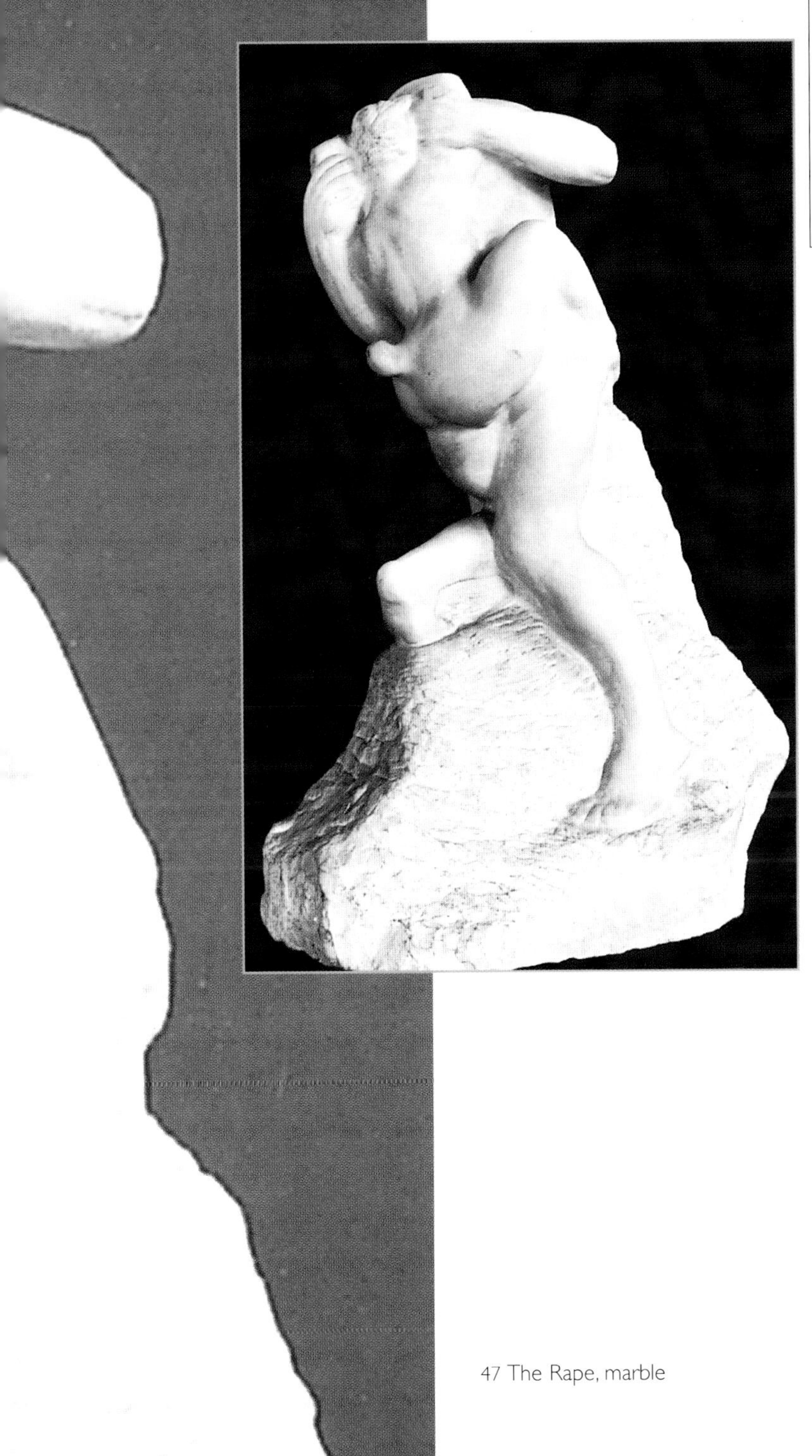

47 The Rape, marble

the Church and the buildings given over to a convent. In the aftermath of the political and social divisions thrown up by the Dreyfus affair, the French state had formally separated from the Church. As part of this process much church land was repossessed. The Hôtel Biron was in a dilapidated condition and the government let it out at low rents. Artists and other more bohemian types rented the old rooms as apartments or studios. The plumbing was hopeless, heating no better; and in the huge, completely overgrown grounds wild rabbits (rather appropriately) expended their natural energies without check or hindrance. At various times during this colourful period Rodin's fellow tenants included the dramatist Jean Cocteau, the painter Henri Matisse, the German poet Rainer Maria Rilke (at one time Rodin's private secretary and author of a superb monograph on him), Isadora Duncan and a flamboyant, homosexual actor called Edouard du Max.

Du Max converted the sacristy of the convent's chapel into his bathroom; rumours of the nature of Rodin's drawings and of the behaviour of his models, and other scandalous goings-on seeped into the press. Diaghilev

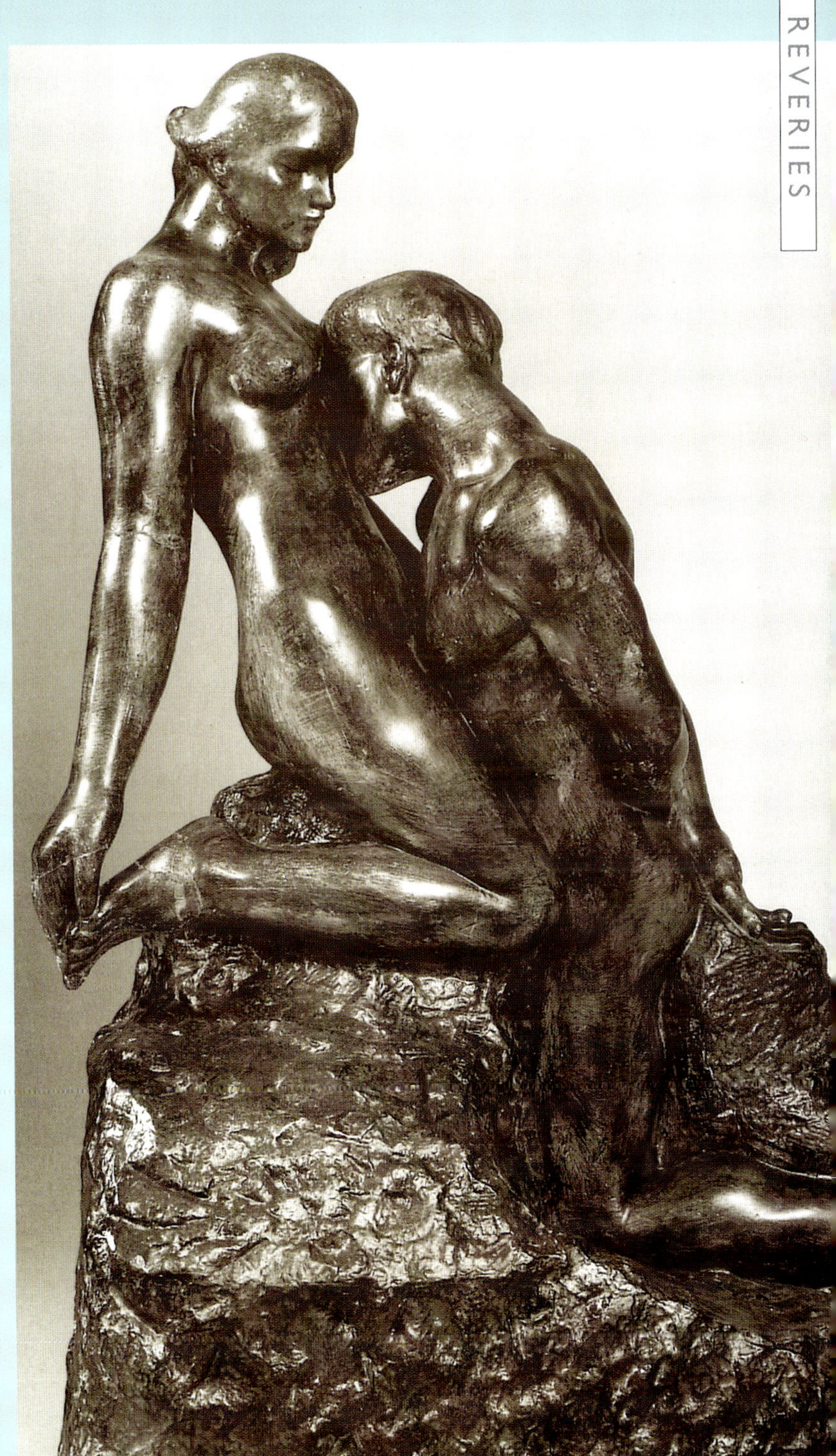

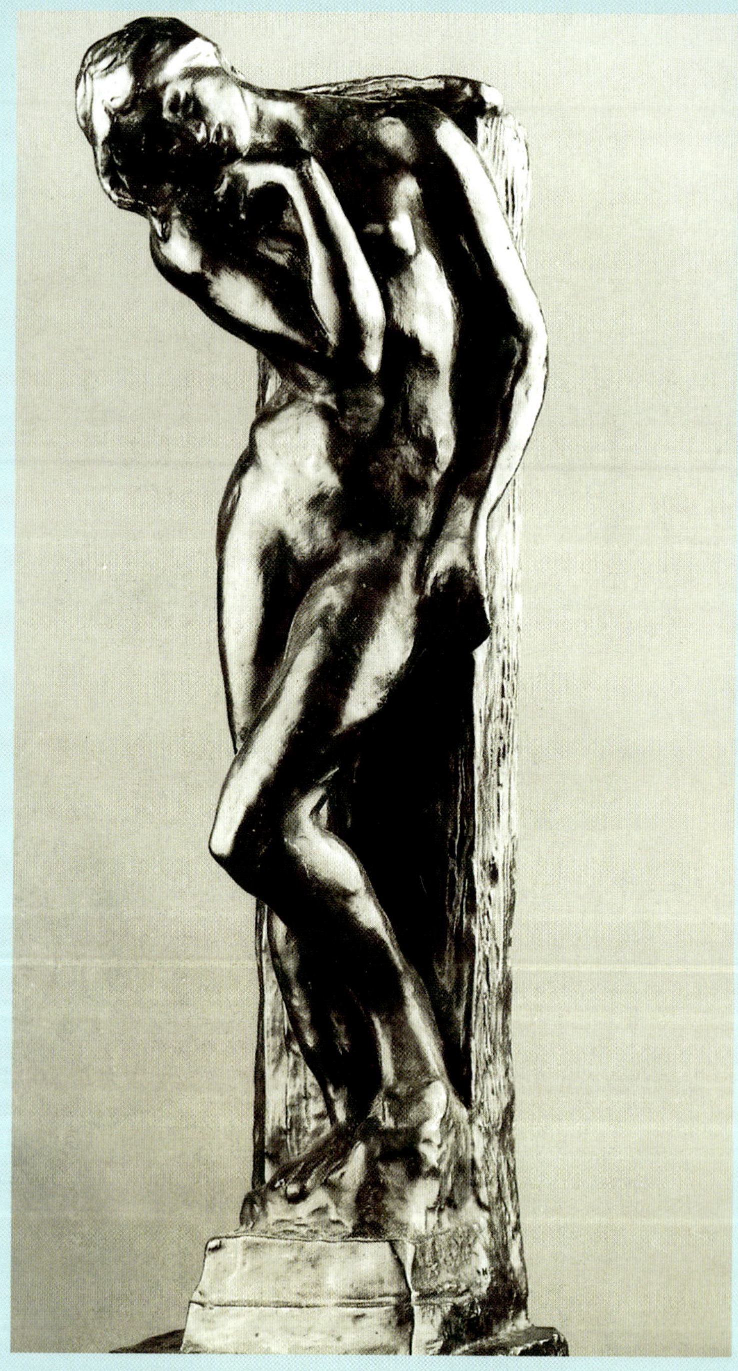

49 Eve at the pillar

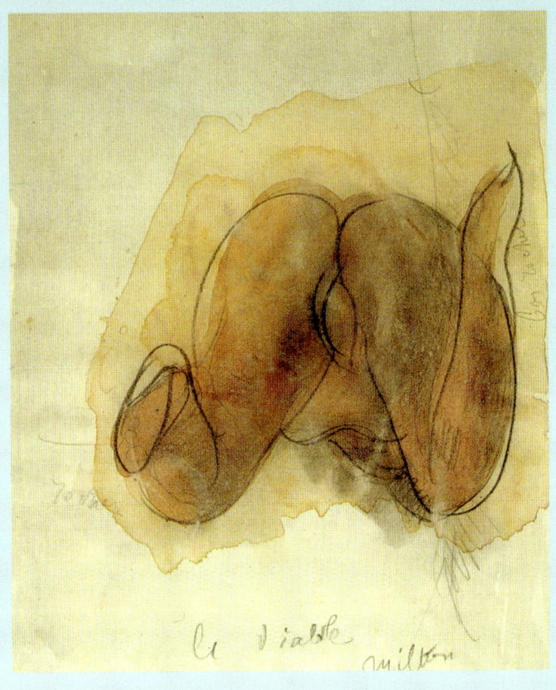

50 The Devil or Milton, 1900, lead and watercolour

found Rodin and Nijinsky fast asleep on the unkempt lawn one afternoon in 1912, after a bibulous lunch; and he circulated reports that Rodin and the dancer were having an affair. There were calls to close the place down. The Hôtel Biron is now the Musée Rodin. Only a fraction of the total number of late erotic drawings are now normally hung together on its walls.

REACTIONS

Responses to these works have been varied. When a small number of them were shown in Cologne at an exhibition in 1906, the director of the museum concerned was forced to resign because of the furore that ensued. Rodin, as a result, became wary of showing these drawings in public. They were for the most part private works which have only slowly and fitfully entered the public realm. They have attracted

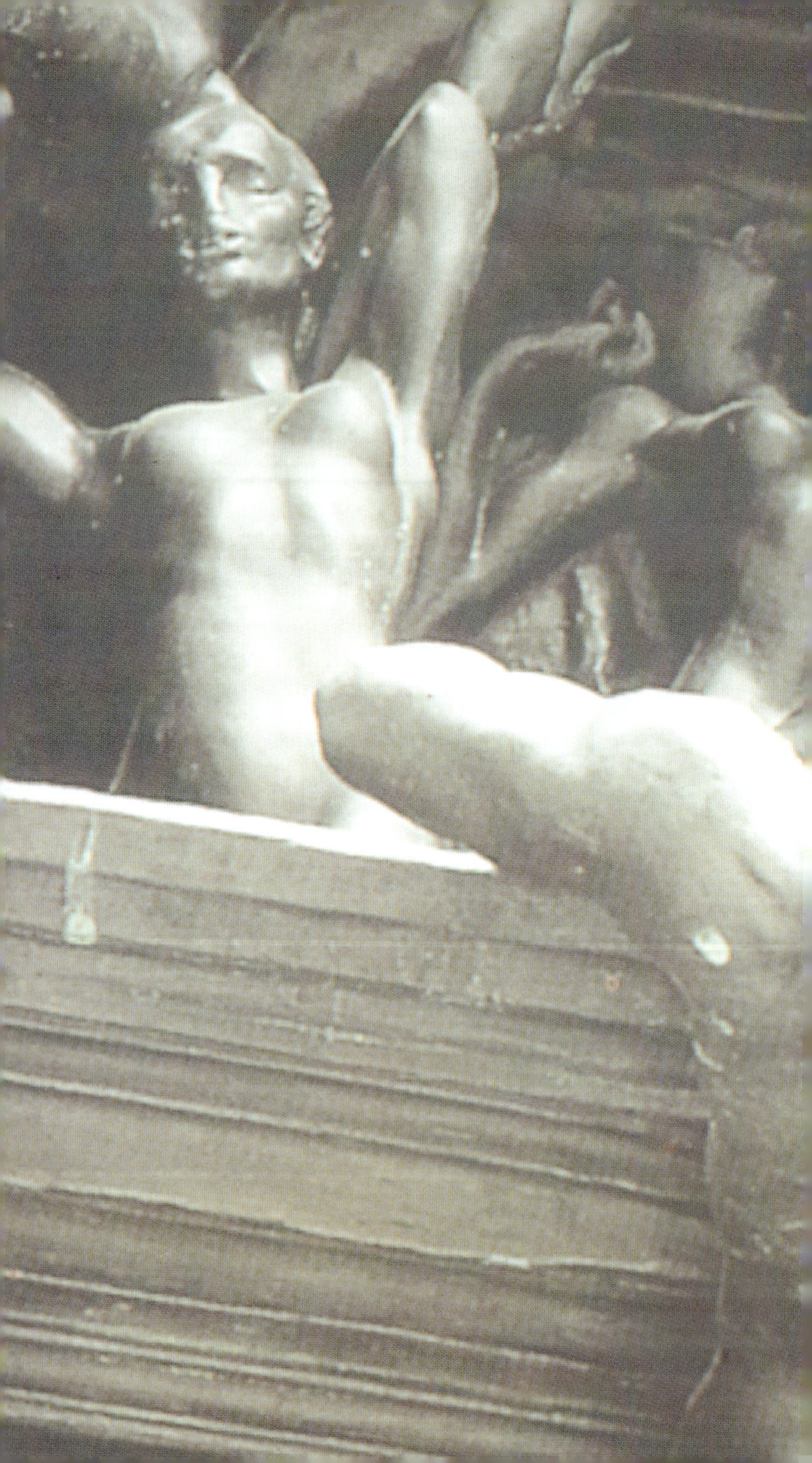

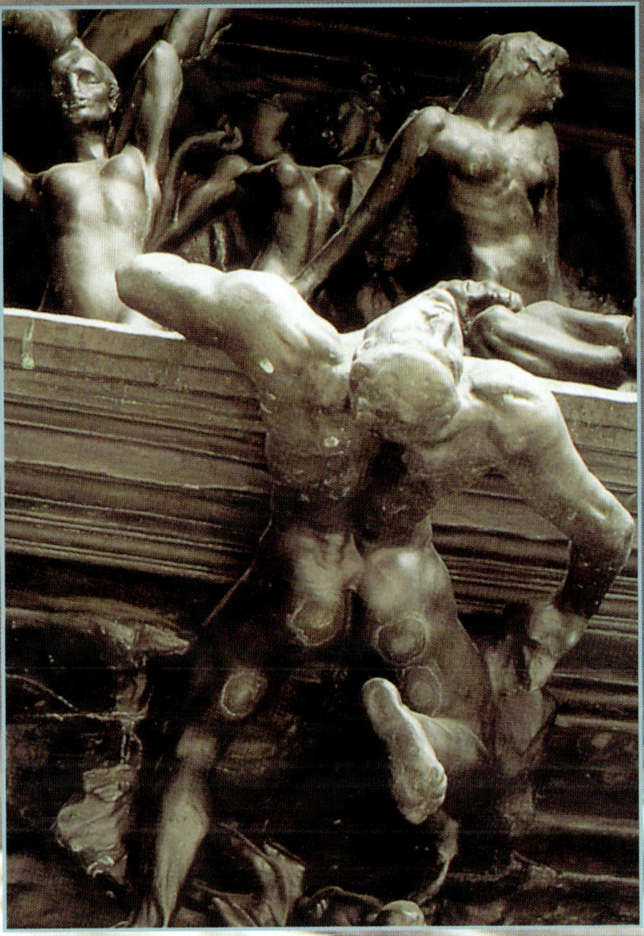

51 - The Gates of Hell

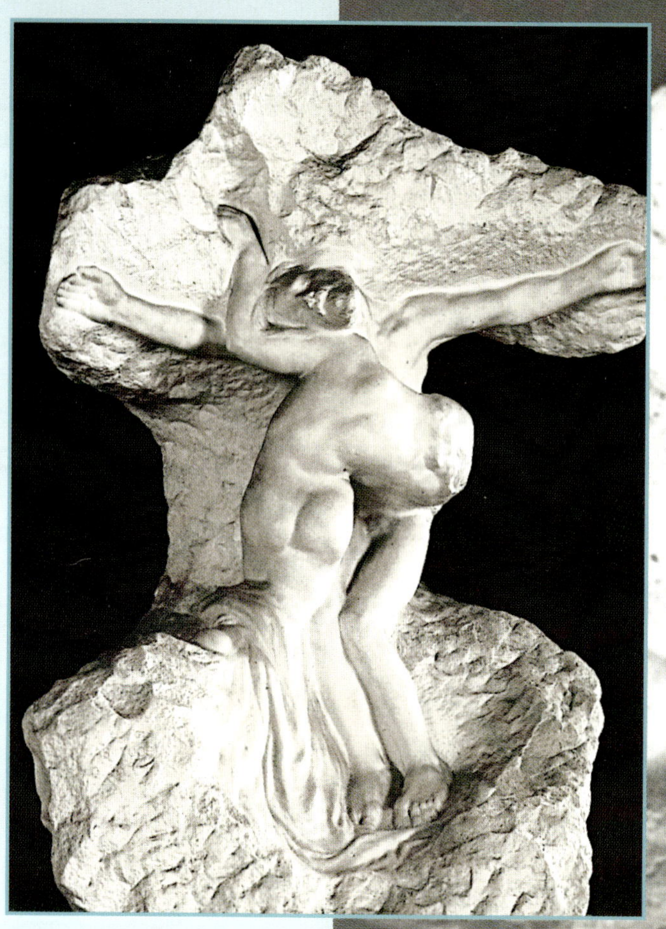

52 Christ and Mary Magdalene, 1894, marble

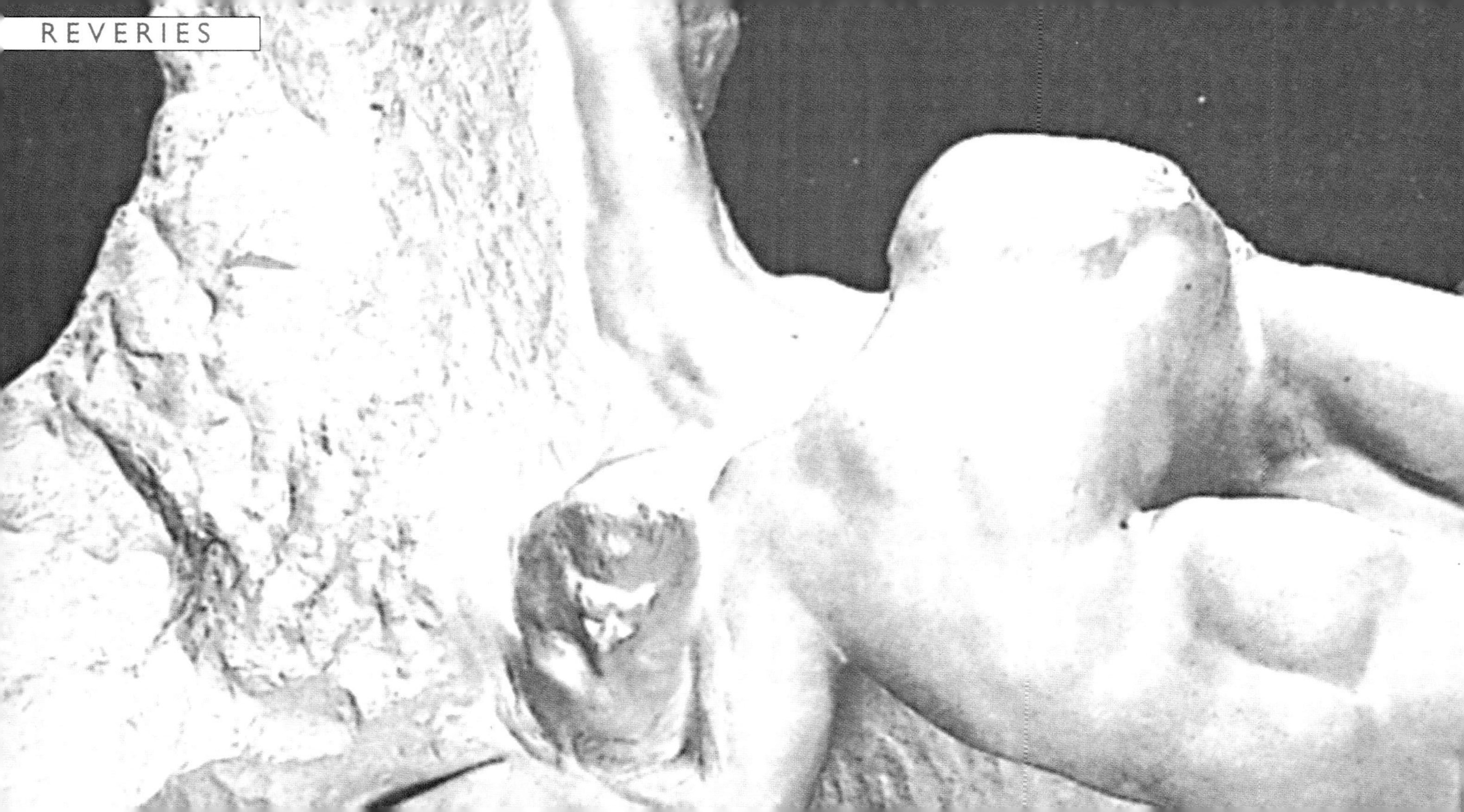

charges of voyeurism and of being merely the fantasies of an impotent old man and they have been dismissed as pornographic.

The voyeuristic element is undeniable - the models are not posed so as to solicit any suspension of disbelief in the way, by contrast, that Degas's late nude pastels do: portraying models as lone women washing in the privacy of the bathroom. Degas's models appear to be being spied upon ("through the keyhole" as he put it), while Rodin's figures are clearly only, just models - performing and taking their own enjoyment in front of the artist.

The American curator Kirk Varnedoe has described how the process of viewing many hundreds of these drawings together at the other Musée Rodin at Meudon led him through a series of different reactions: surprise, amusement, astonishment, tedium. "Finally", he continues, "I find all my skepticisms defeated. These are not documents of idle self-indulgence, but of heated, driving fascination. The recurrent themes of death and the conflicts of consciousness that compelled the young man's work have here been supplanted, in the spirit of the aging artist, by an ecstatic obsession with the mystery of creation taken at its primal source." The comparison struck between the younger and older

53
The Hand of God, 1897, marble

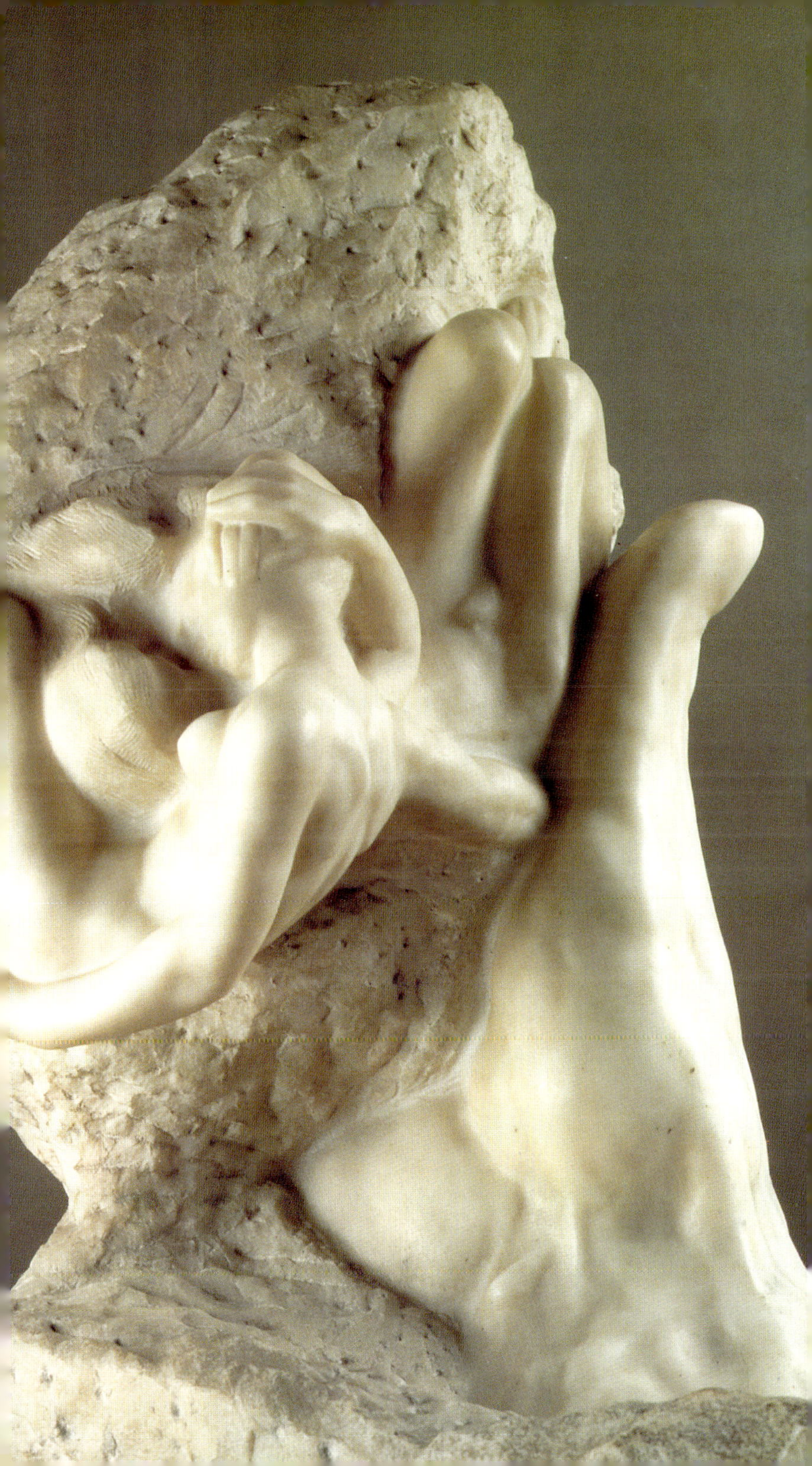

Rodin's work is an interesting one - as if his oeuvre charted a journey in which the earlier obsession with death and suffering is transformed into something very different: a journey from a state of spiritual claustrophobia and struggle to one of liberation and celebration, a journey from the gates of hell to the doors of life.

If such an interpretation is valid then the issues of voyeurism, male fantasy and the pornographic (with which these drawings have been and are enmeshed) seem to locate themselves, so to speak, less problematically in the background. Rodin himself is recorded as saying towards the end of his life: "I feel beauty in all its manifestations. the wonder of it over-

54 Gates of Hell, right hand pillar detail, bronze

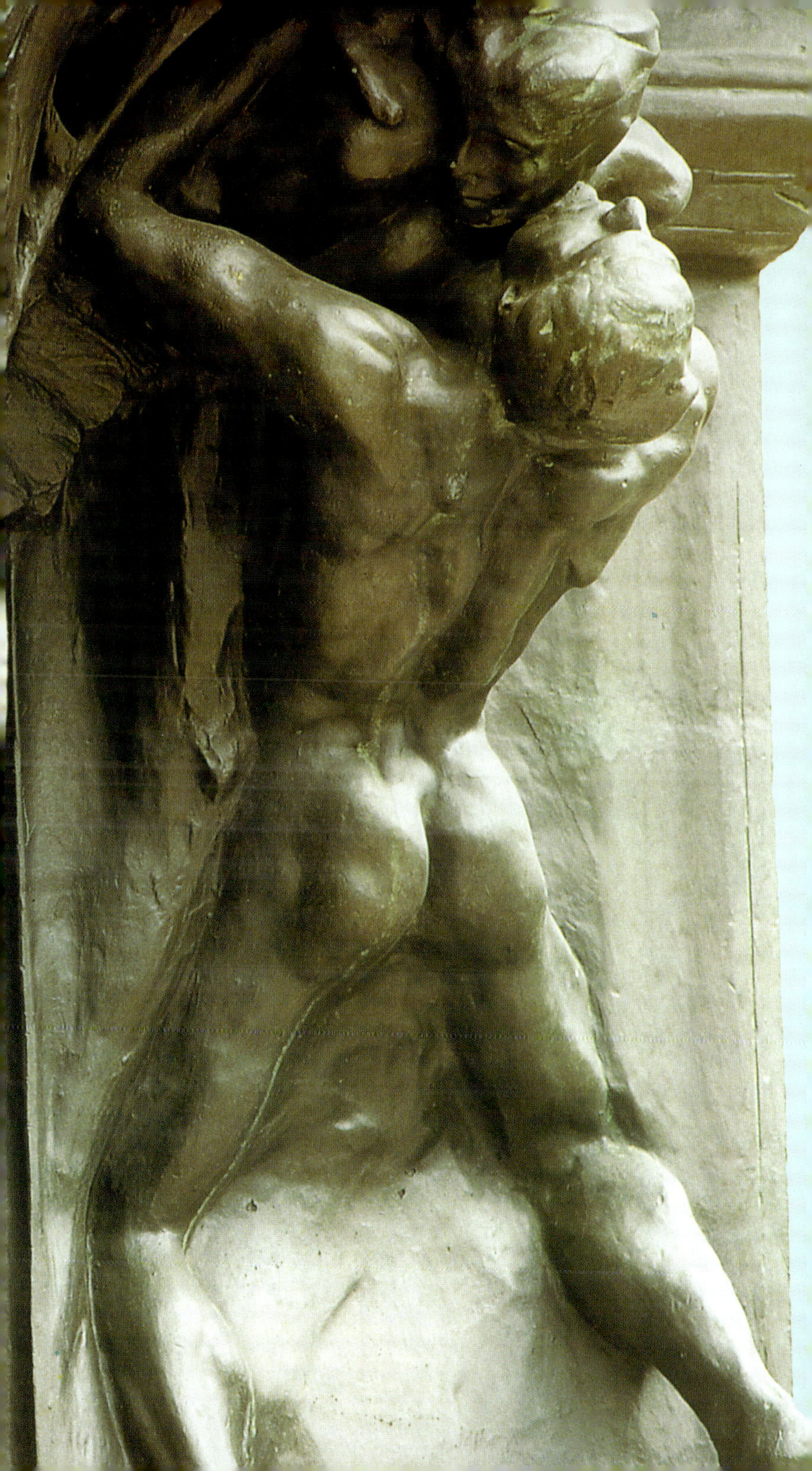

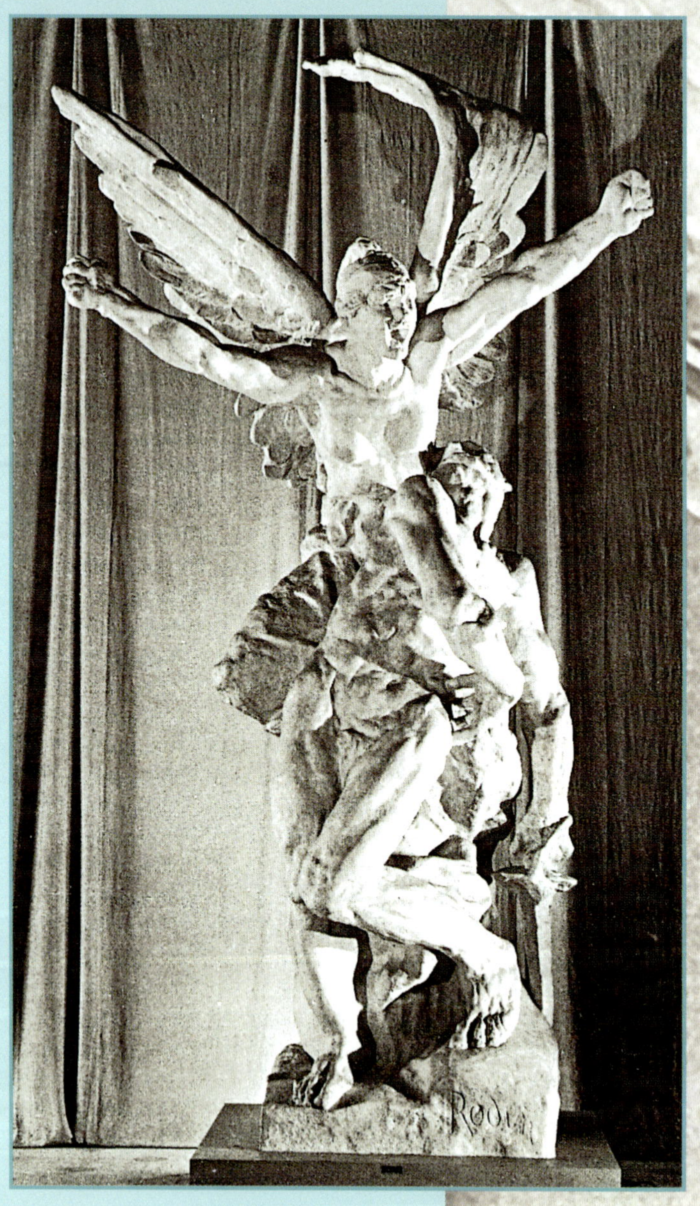

55 Call to Arms, marble,

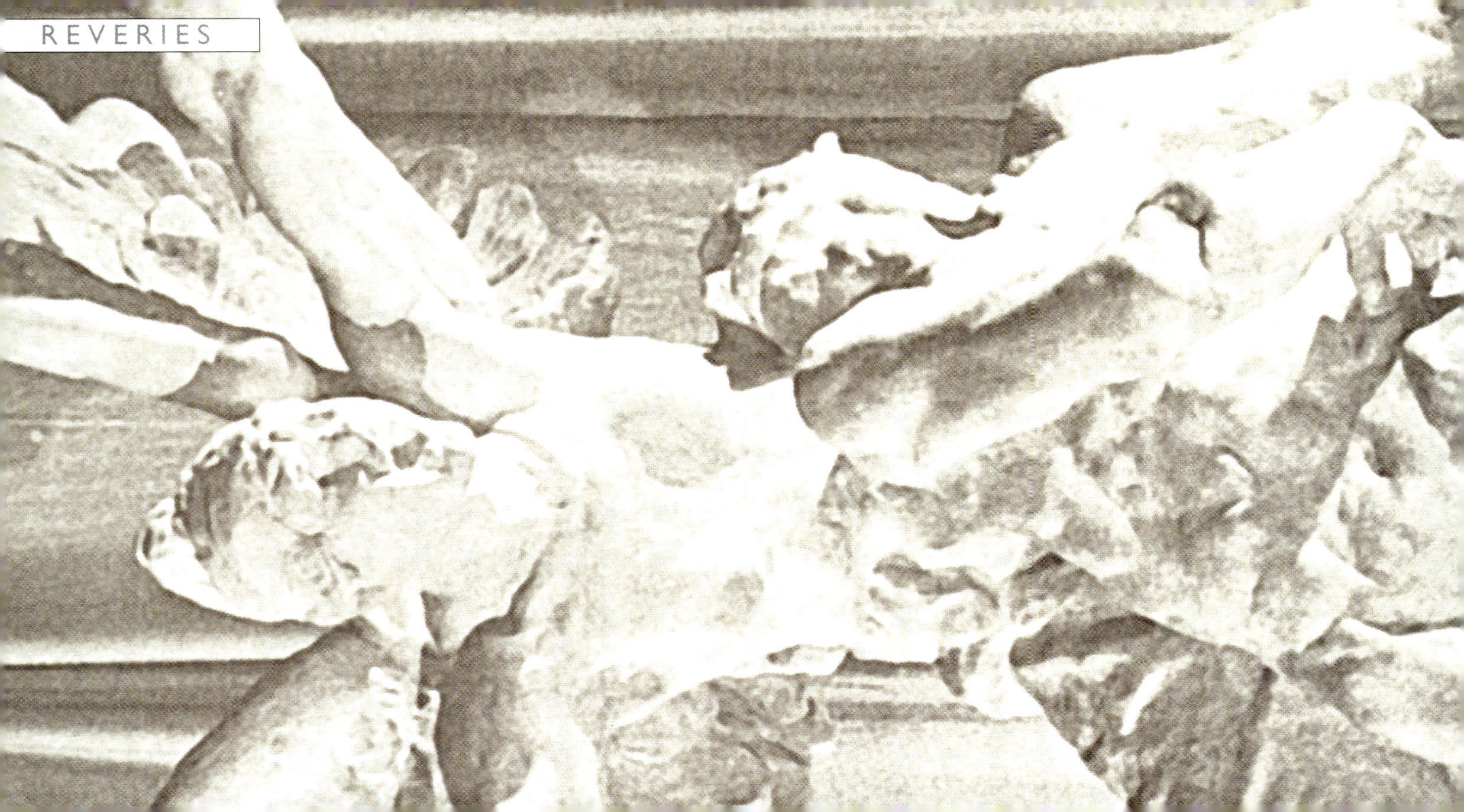

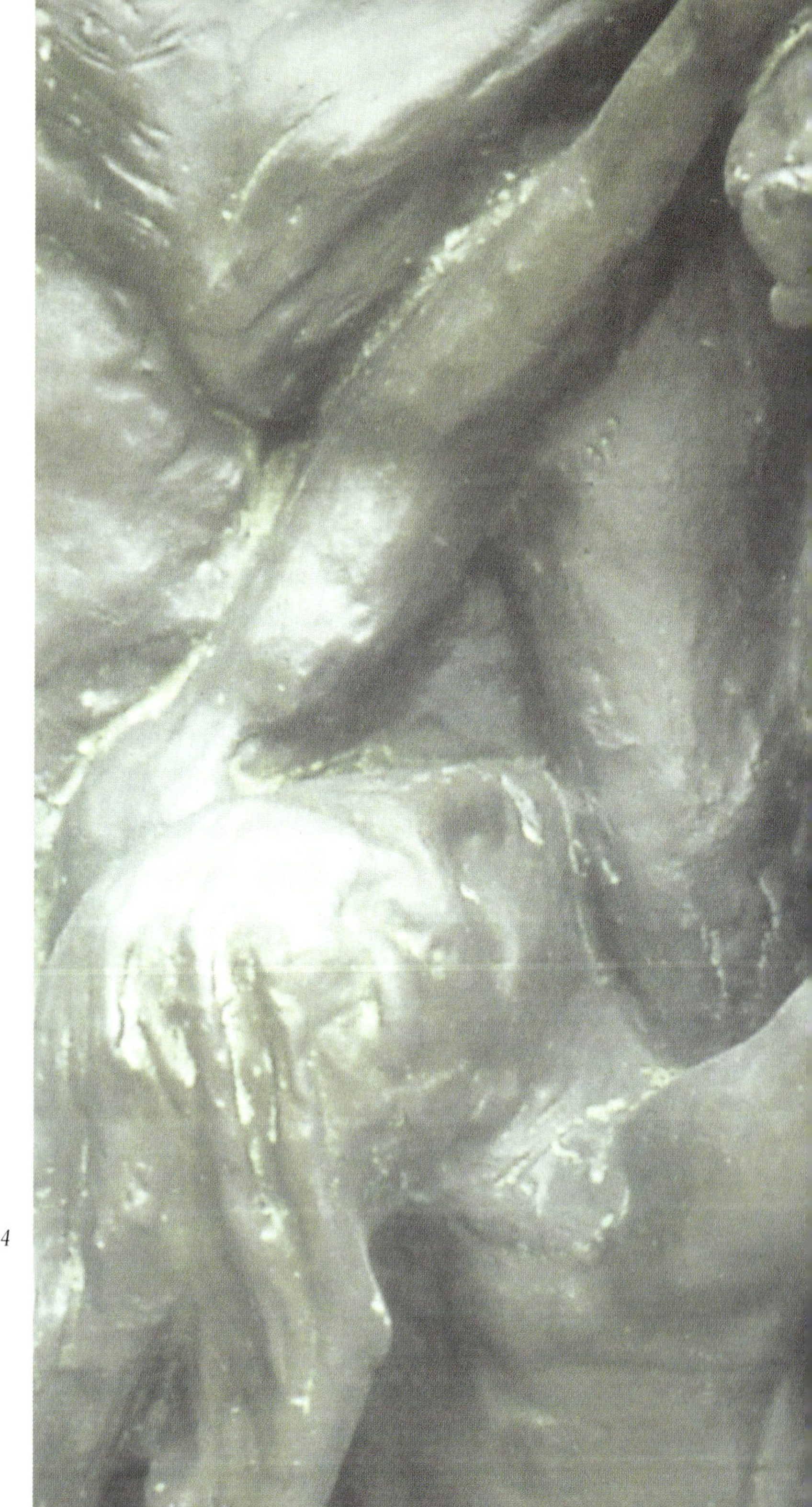

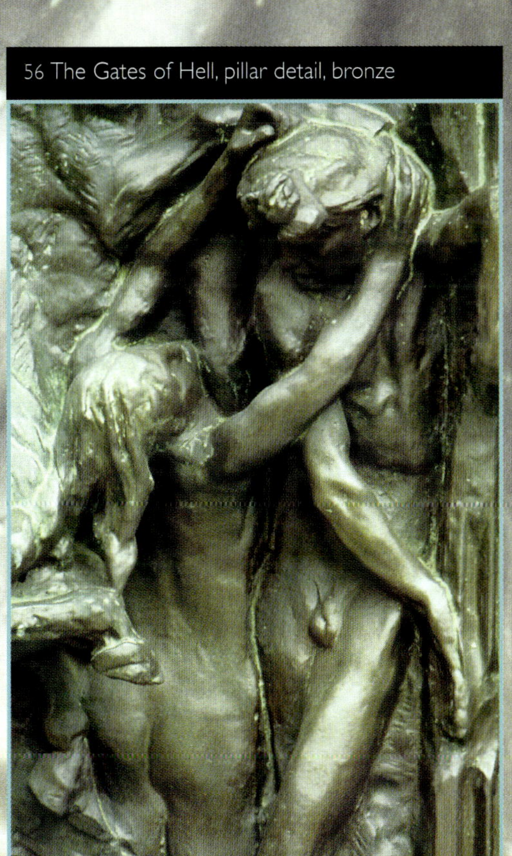

56 The Gates of Hell, pillar detail, bronze

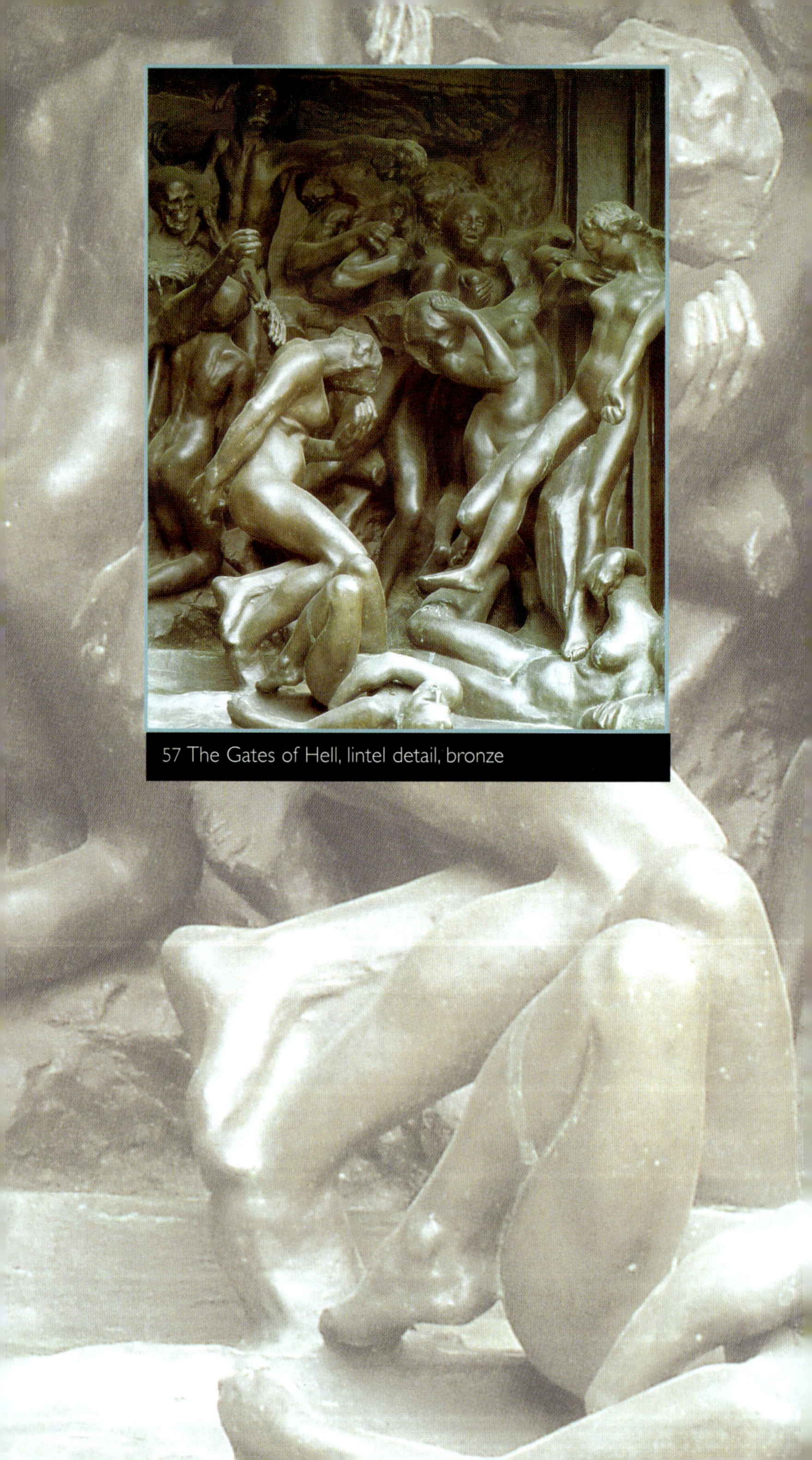

57 The Gates of Hell, lintel detail, bronze

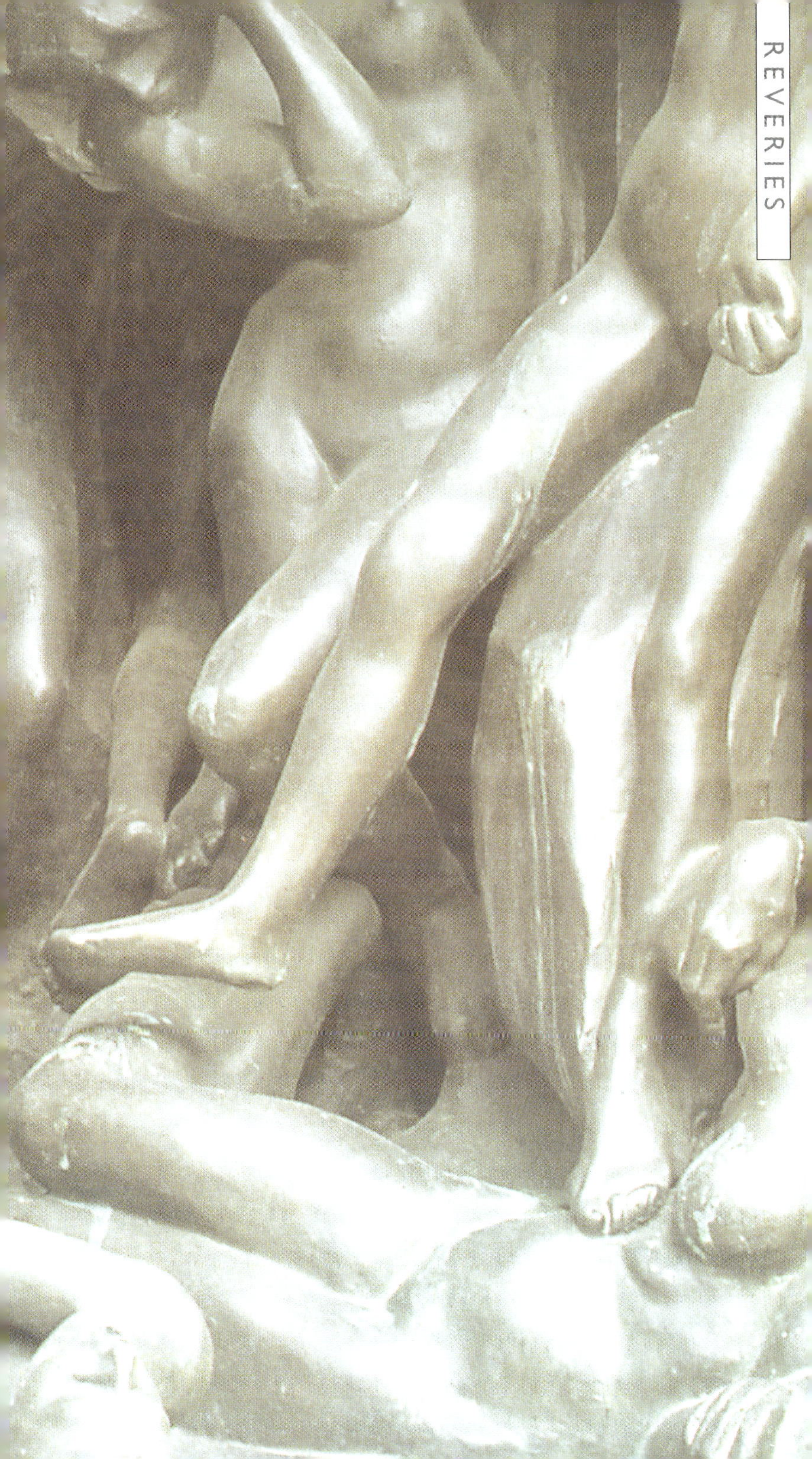

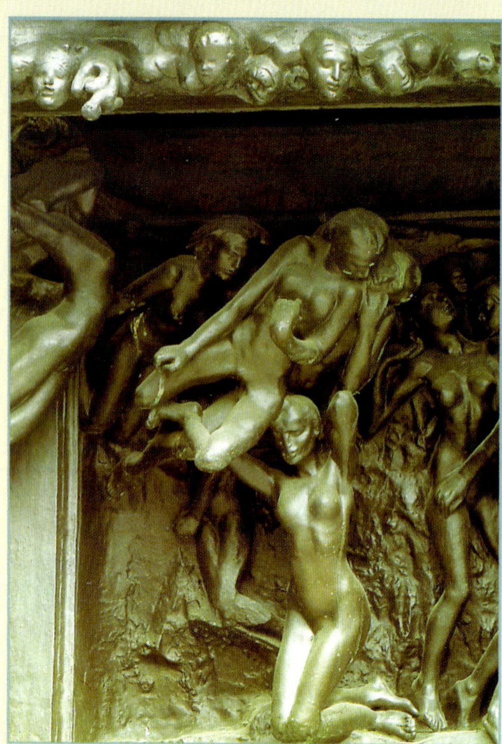

58 The Gates of Hell, lintel detail, bronze

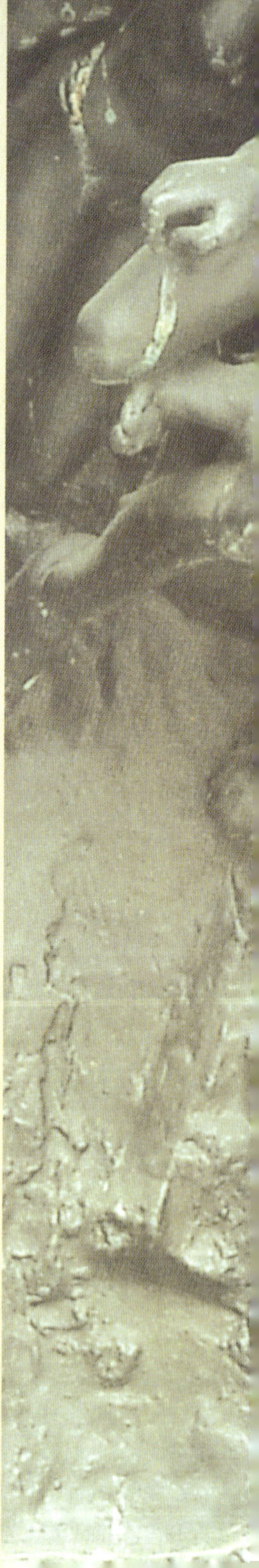

whelms me afresh every day. I am going to die - I must die - but I am like a tree in full flowering." When read with the drawings in mind, Rodin's remarks imply that there is something affirmative, creative, uninhibited and joyous within our erotic selves that need not be felt, as it was often enough earlier in his career, as oppressive, febrile or frustrated.

Such a view of Rodin's oeuvre as a whole would place the vitality of the *Balzac* and the late drawings against the morbidity of the *Gates* and many of the pre-1900 sculptures. It does seem, in retrospect, that it was working on the *Balzac* monument

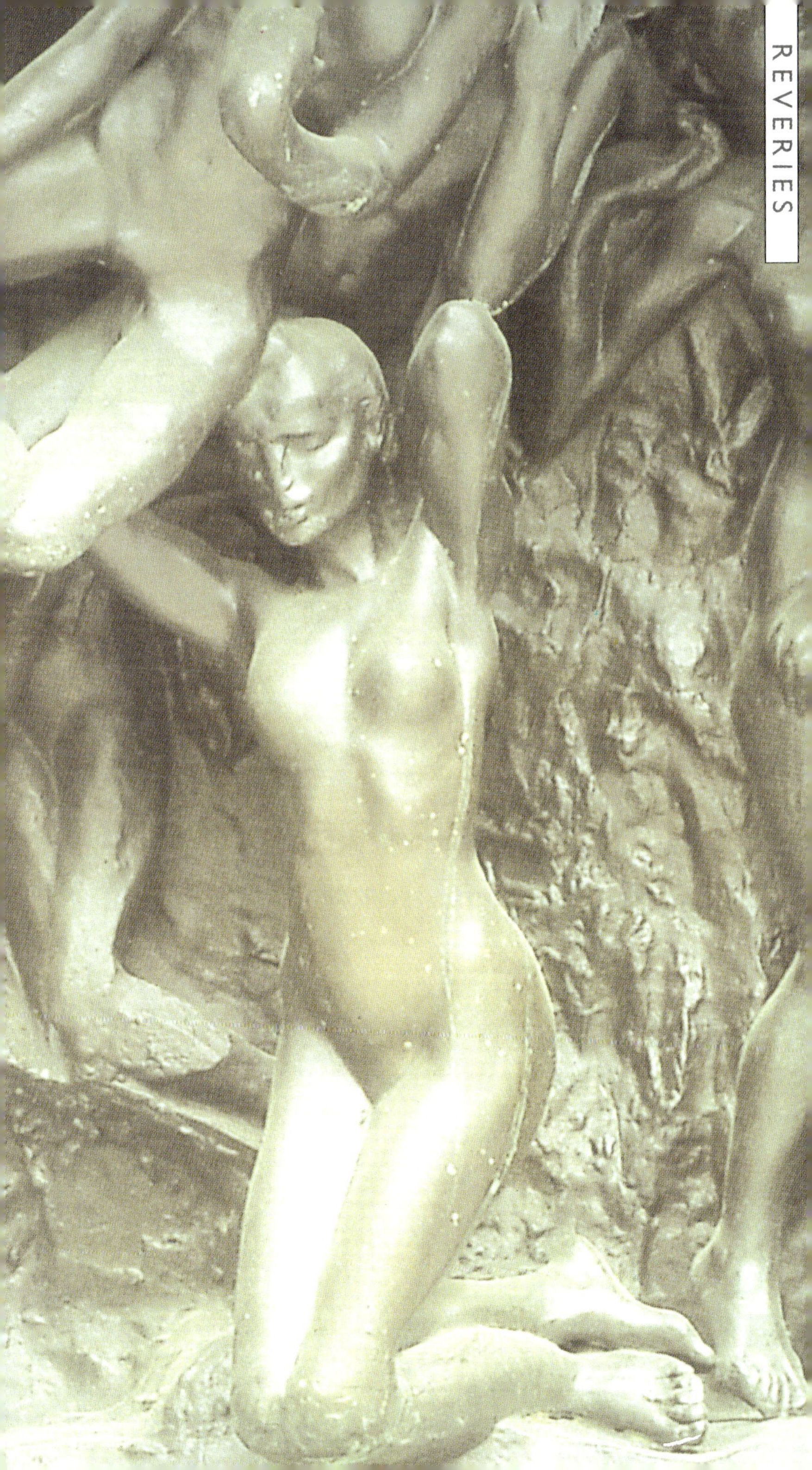

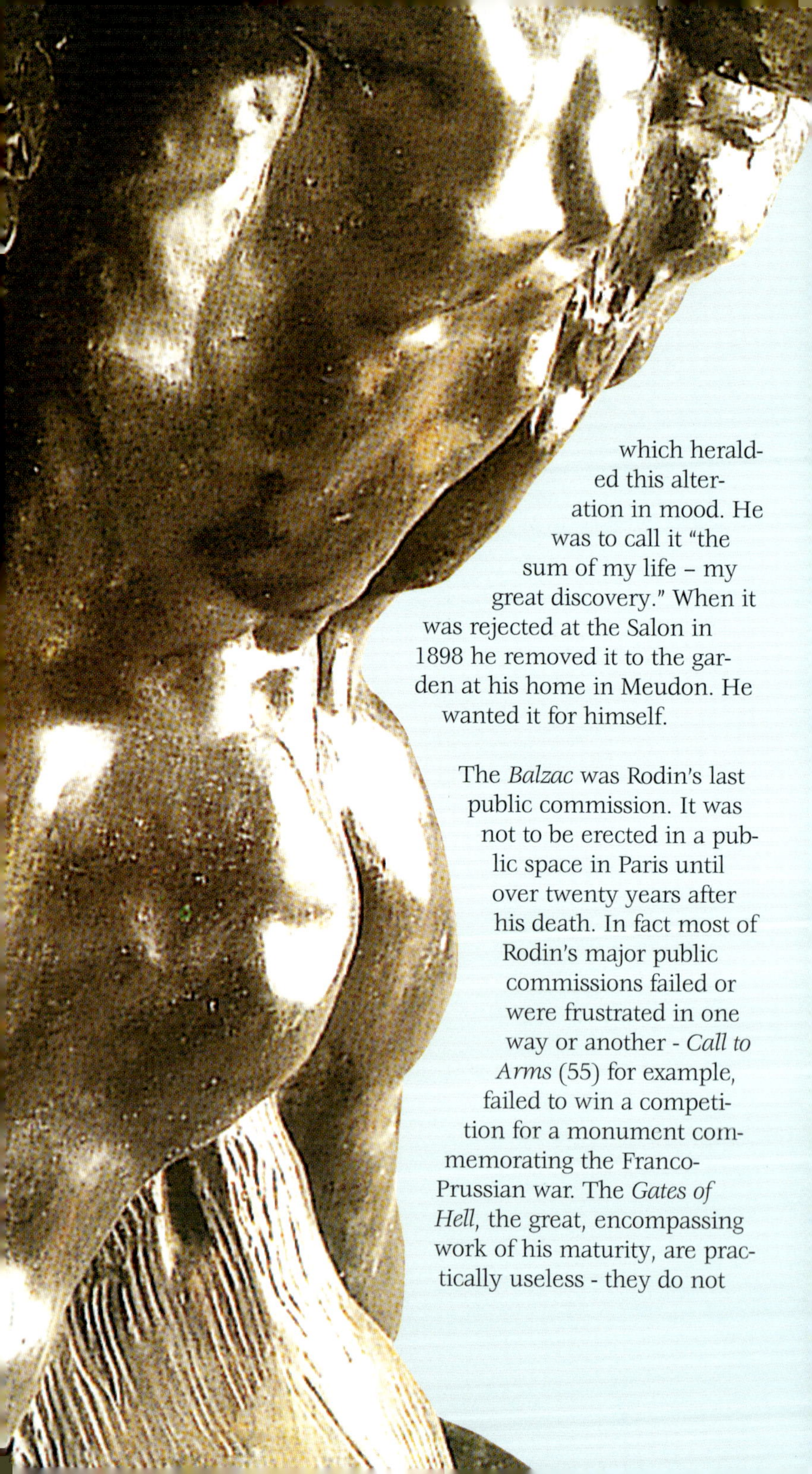

which heralded this alteration in mood. He was to call it "the sum of my life – my great discovery." When it was rejected at the Salon in 1898 he removed it to the garden at his home in Meudon. He wanted it for himself.

The *Balzac* was Rodin's last public commission. It was not to be erected in a public space in Paris until over twenty years after his death. In fact most of Rodin's major public commissions failed or were frustrated in one way or another - *Call to Arms* (55) for example, failed to win a competition for a monument commemorating the Franco-Prussian war. The *Gates of Hell*, the great, encompassing work of his maturity, are practically useless - they do not

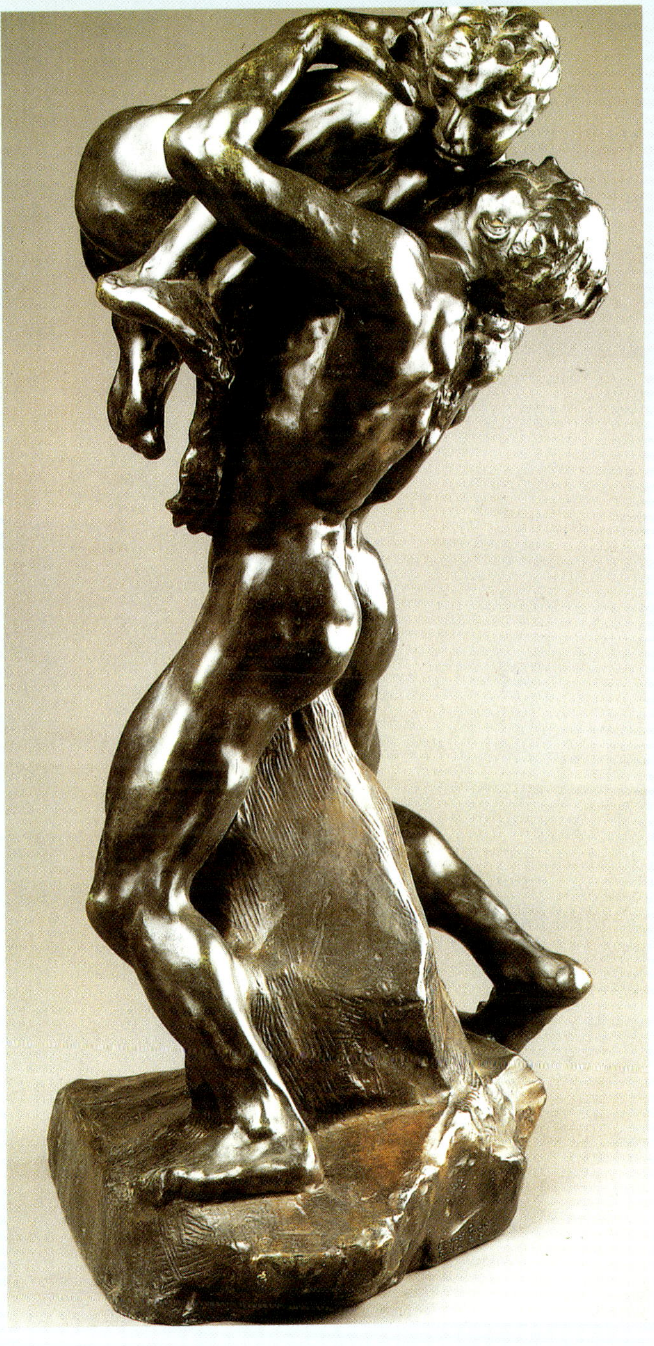

59 I am beautiful, 1882, bronze, Musée Rodin, Paris

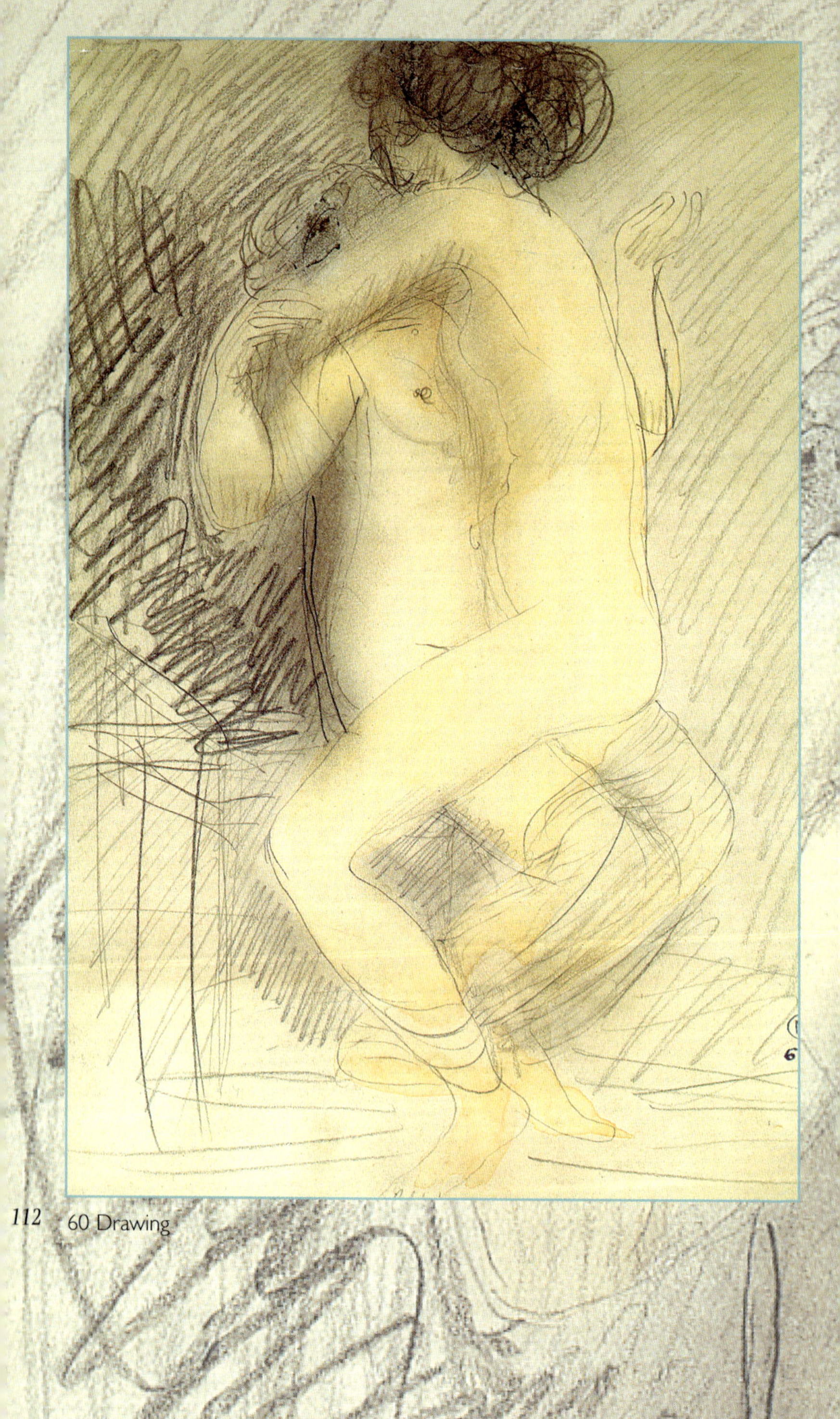

60 Drawing

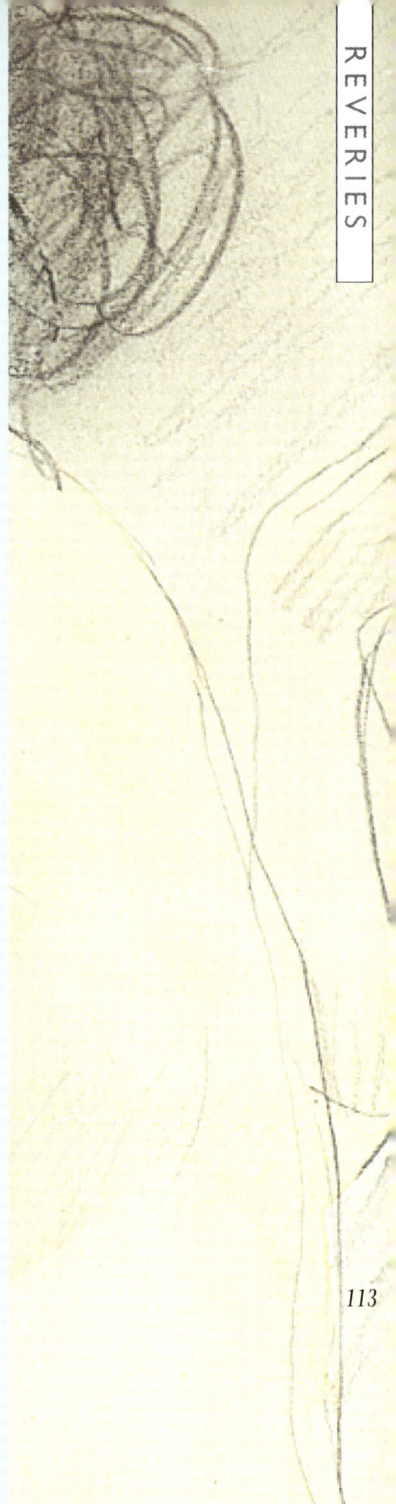

open. The museum for which they were commissioned was never built (what is now the Musée d'Orsay was built in its place). They were not cast in bronze in his lifetime. Neither was Rodin ever paid in full for his work.

Even so, taking his oeuvre as a whole, the range of erotic experience with which it engages is enormous. From conflict, estrangement, struggle and despair, from violence (*The Rape* - 47) and seductive grief (Christ and *Mary Magdalene* - 52) to the liberation and energy of the last drawings: it is as if all human emotion could be conceived in erotic terms. A decidedly iconoclastic twentieth century artist, Jean Arp, wrote a short poetic tribute to Rodin in which he lamented the advent of what he called the "Mechanical erotomachy of our century", comparing this development wistfully against Rodin's more humane achievements within an erotic sphere.

So as not to be disturbed, Rodin himself used to pin a notice to

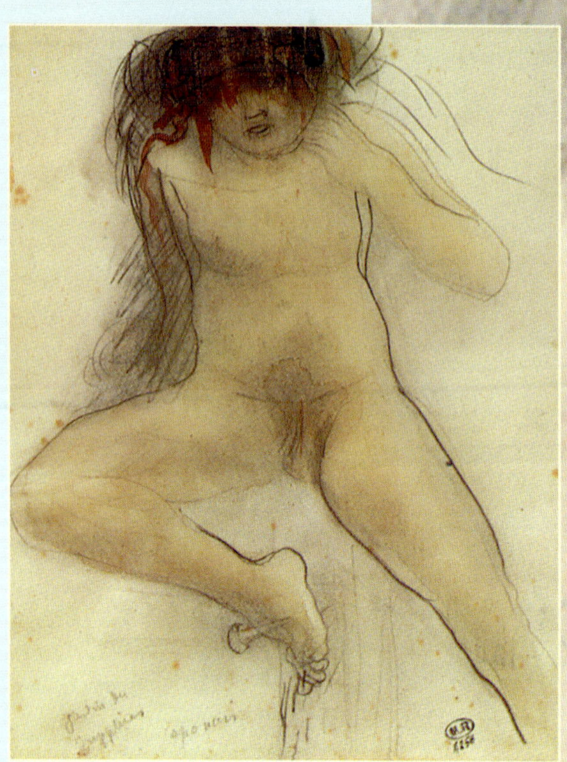

61 Garden of Pain. 1898
graphite, stump and watercolour on buff paper, Musée Rodin, Paris

the door of his studio when otherwise engaged with one of his models: "Monsieur Rodin is away visiting cathedrals." And in a figurative sense the statement was not untruthful. For the human body, in particular the female, was a temple for him (6). "The dazzling splendour revealed to the artist by the model that

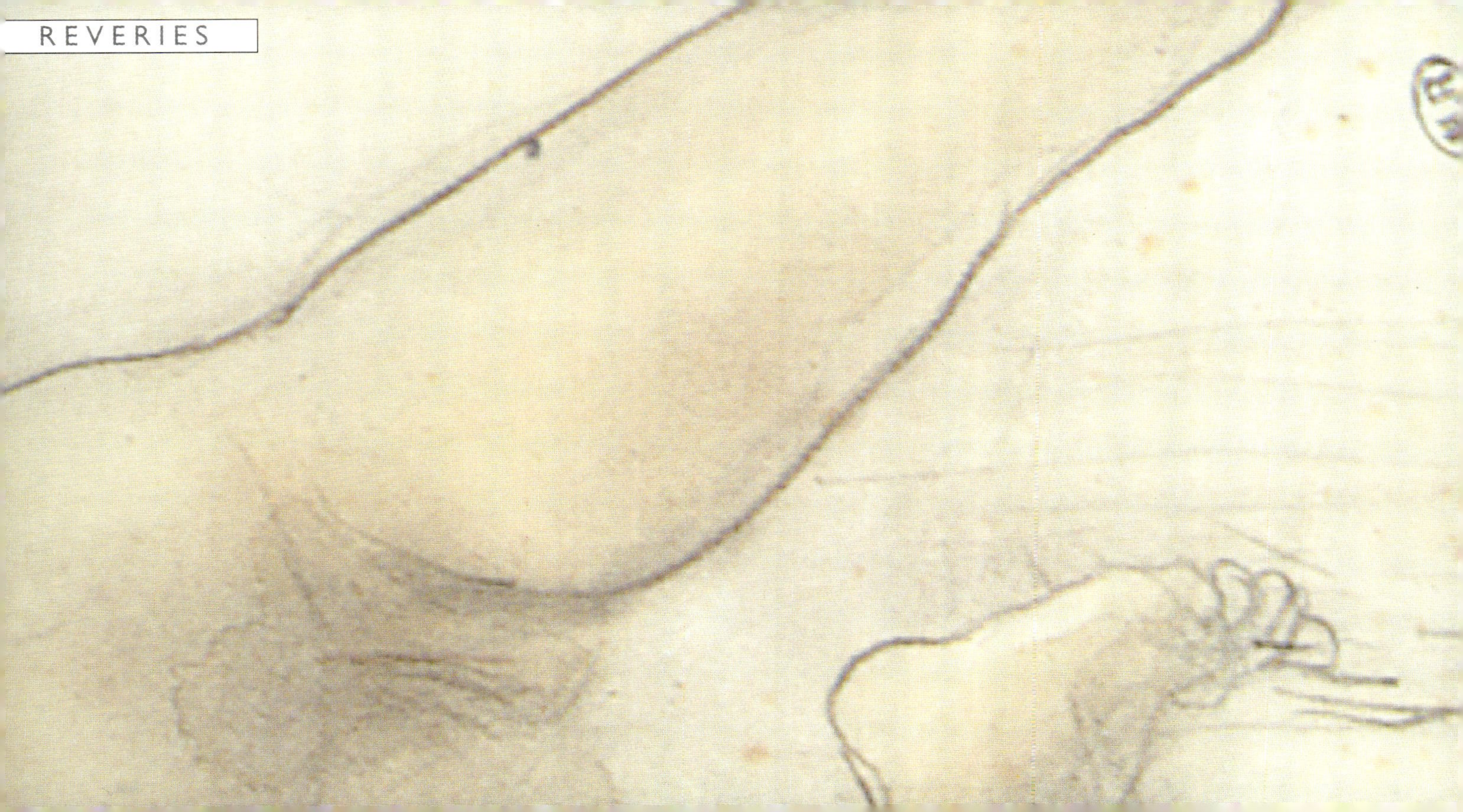

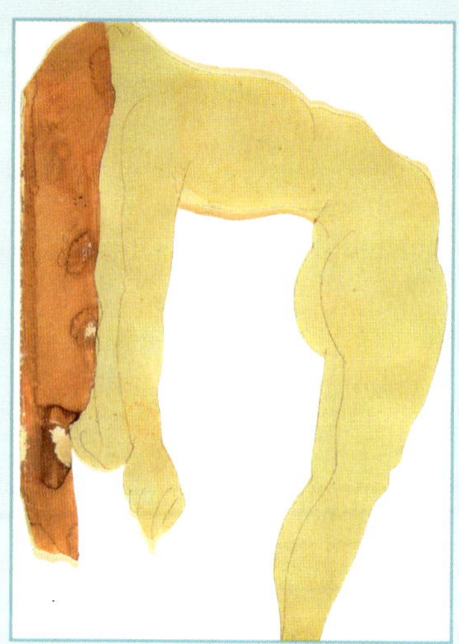

62 Female nude with long hair leaning backwards, graphite and watercolour on cut-out buff paper. Musée Rodin, Paris

divests herself of her clothes has the effect of the sun piercing the clouds. Venus, Eve, these are feeble terms to express the beauty of woman", he is recorded as saying by his earliest biographer. As is clear in the way he composed the *Gates*, Rodin did not feel obliged to follow any paths set down already by literature. In fact, in other works he often only added literary or mythological titles once the figures had already been modelled (10). On occasion he seems deliberately to have ignored his literary source: in *Hand of God* (53), Rodin models the divine hand caressing Woman or Eve into existence; she is born, not from Adam's rib, but as an independent creature in her own right. From the forthright advances of Francesca in *The Kiss* (1), to the man's submission before his muse in *Eternal Idol* (7) and, finally, in the late erotic drawings it seems that, perhaps, the most relevant legacy the erotic explorations of his work (if not his life) have left us is this: of woman as the sexual equal of man.

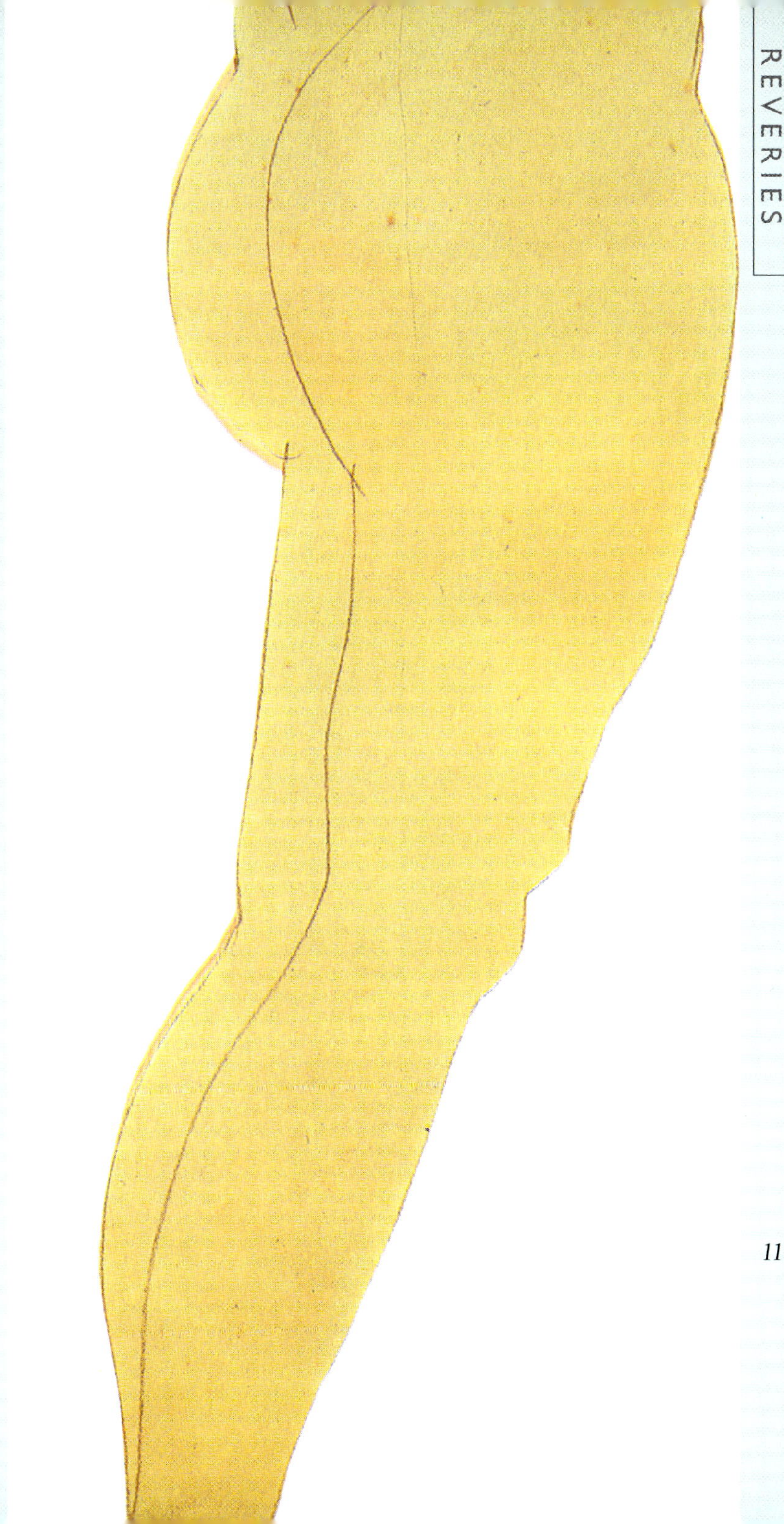

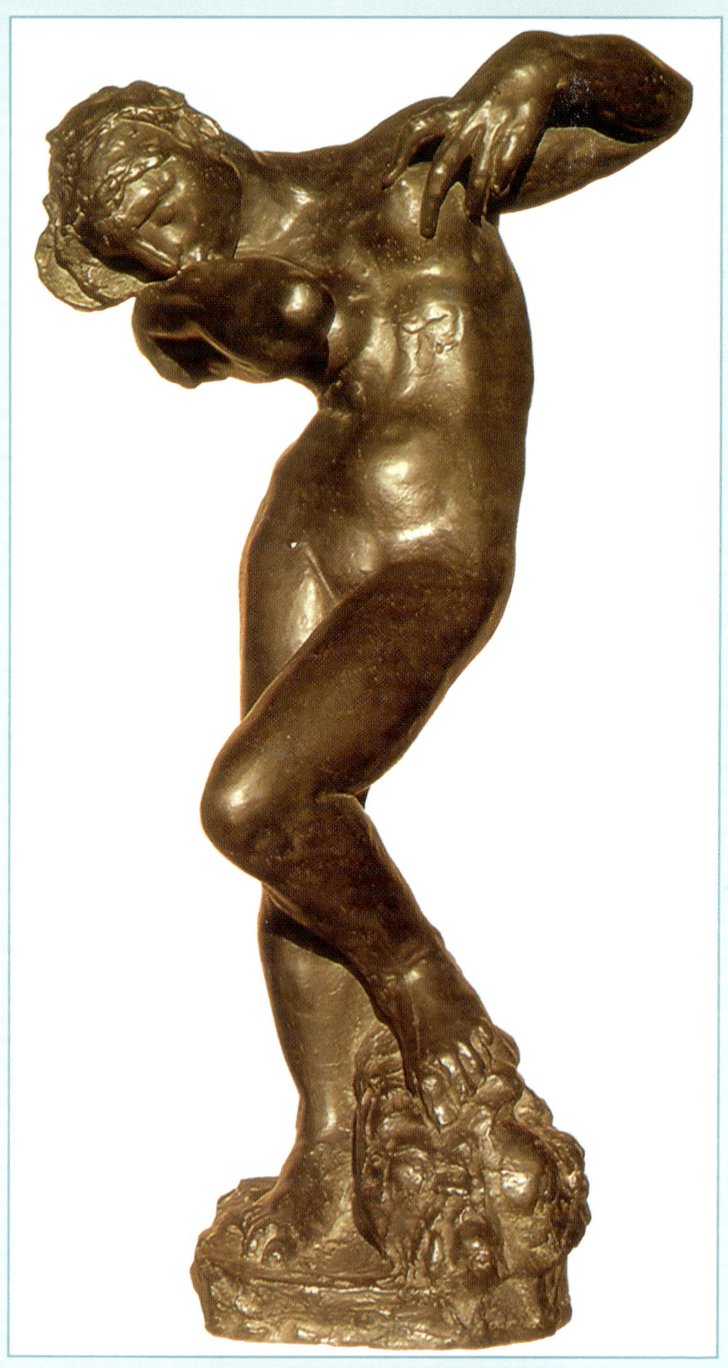

PICTURE LIST

1 The Kiss Page 5
2 Balzac, marble Page 7
3 The Gates of Hell Page 9
4 Torso of a Young Woman Page 10
5 Dawn Page 12
24 Sapphic couple near the wheel of fortune Page 14
7 Eternal idol Page 16
8 Fugit Amor, circa 1890, bronze Page 18
9 Paolo and Fransesca, 1887, bronze Page 21
10 Vertumnus and Pommona, 1905, marble Page 23
11 The Tempest, marble Page 25
12 The Toilet of Venus, bronze Page 27
13 The Temple of Love, lead and watercolour Page 28
14 Salammbô Page 31
15 Hand on a woman's sex, lead and charcoal Page 33
16 Jean-Baptisite Rodin, father of the artist Page 35
17 Hélène Nostitz, circa 1902, plaster Page 36
18 Rose Beuret, circa 1890, bronze Page 37
19 Eternal Spring, 1884, marble Page 39
20 Danaid Page 41
21 Danaid Page 42
22 Meditiation Page 44
24 Torso of Adèle Page 49
52 Thought Page 52
23 Torso of Adèle Page 49
25 Crouching woman, 1880-82, bronze Page 50
56 La pensée, 1886 Page 52
27 Drawing Page 54
28 Drawing Page 56
29 Before creation, 1990, watercolour Page 58
30 Entwined couple, (The War of love) Page 60
31 Woman on her back, 1990 Page 62
32 Nude woman - on her back, lead on paper Page 65
33 Nude woman on her back, 1900 Page 66
34 Nude woman lying on her stomach Page 68
35 Nude woman holding her thighs Page 70
36 Bust of a nude woman, lead on paper Page 72
37 Drawing Page 74
38 Courtesan Page 76
39 Iris, Messenger of the Gods, bronze Page 78
40 Cambodian dancer, 1906 Page 80
41 Reclining woman with a bird, 1910 Page 81
42 Cambodian dancer, 1906 Page 82
43 Drawing Page 83
44 Brother and Sister Page 84
45 I am Beautiful, 1882, marble Page 86
46 Hanako Page 87
47 The Rape, marble Page 88
48 Eternal idol, 1889 Page 90
49 The Devil or Milton, 1900, lead and watercolour Page 93
50 Eve at the pillar, bronze Page 92
51 The Gates of Hell, detail Page 94
52 Christ and Mary Magdalene Page 96
53 The Hand of God, 1887, marble Page 98
54 The Gates of Hell, detail Page 100
55 Call to Arms Page 102
56 The Gates of Hell, detail Page 104
57 The Gates of Hell, detail Page 106
58 The Gates of Hell, detail Page 108
59 I am beautiful, 1882, bronze Page 110
60 Drawing Page 112
61 Garden of Pain, 1898 Page 114
62 Female nude with long hair Page 116